CONSTRUCTING EXILE

CONSTRUCTING EXILE

The Emergence of a Biblical Paradigm

JOHN HILL, CSSR

CASCADE *Books* • Eugene, Oregon

CONSTRUCTING EXILE
The Emergence of a Biblical Paradigm

Copyright © 2020 John Hill, CSSR. All rights reserved. Except for brief quotations in critical publications or reviews, no part of this book may be reproduced in any manner without prior written permission from the publisher. Write: Permissions, Wipf and Stock Publishers, 199 W. 8th Ave., Suite 3, Eugene, OR 97401.

Cascade Books
An Imprint of Wipf and Stock Publishers
199 W. 8th Ave., Suite 3
Eugene, OR 97401

www.wipfandstock.com

PAPERBACK ISBN: 978-1-7252-5499-2
HARDCOVER ISBN: 978-1-7252-5500-5
EBOOK ISBN: 978-1-7252-5501-2

Cataloguing-in-Publication data:

Names: Hill, John, 1948–, author.

Title: Constructing exile : the emergence of a biblical paradigm / John Hill, CSSR.

Description: Eugene, OR: Cascade Books, 2020 | Includes bibliographical references and index.

Identifiers: ISBN 978-1-7252-5499-2 (paperback) | ISBN 978-1-7252-5500-5 (hardcover) | ISBN 978-1-7252-5501-2 (ebook)

Subjects: LCSH: Jews—History—Babylonian captivity, 598–515 B.C. | Jews—History—Babylonian captivity, 598–515 B.C.—Biblical teaching | Exiles—Psychology | Jews—Restoration | Bible—Old Testament—Criticism, interpretation, etc.

Classification: BS1199.B3 H55 2020 (print) | BS1199.B3 (ebook)

Manufactured in the U.S.A.   JULY 10, 2020

The biblical texts used here are those licensed for use in Bible Works 9 (Bible Works, LLC, 1992–2011). The Hebrew and Greek fonts are those made available by the Society of Biblical Literature (https://www.sbl-site.org/educational/biblicalfonts.aspx).

CONTENTS

Acknowledgements | vii
Abbreviations | ix

Chapter 1: **INTRODUCTION** | 1
    Recent Developments in Research on the Exile | 2
    Exile and Restoration? | 4
    Outline of the Book | 5

Chapter 2: **THE DISASTER OF 587 AND ITS AFTERMATH** | 8
    Setting the Scene: Pre-587 Judah | 8
    Conquest, Dispossession, and Deportations—Biblical Accounts | 11
    Post-587 Judah | 14
    Summary | 17

Chapter 3: **RESPONSES TO THE DISASTER
    —GRIEF AND EXPLANATIONS** | 18
    Grief and the Book of Lamentations | 18
    Explanations of the Disaster | 26
    Summary | 38

Chapter 4: **THE COMMUNITY IN BABYLON
    AND THE EMERGENCE OF HOPE** | 40
    The Crisis of Exile | 41
    Responses to the Crisis | 43
    The Vision of the Future—The End of Exile? | 48
    Summary—Chapter 4 | 63

Chapter 5: **THE EARLY PERSIAN PERIOD
    —FROM EXILE TO RESTORATION?** | 64

The Rise of Cyrus: the Demise of Babylon | 64
   Under Persian Rule | 66
   Exile and Restoration in Haggai and Zech 1–8 | 70
   Exile and Restoration in Ezra and Nehemiah | 77
   Summary | 86

Chapter 6: **THE UNENDED EXILE** | 88
   Isa 56–66 | 88
   The Book of Jeremiah MT | 92
   The Book of Daniel | 97
   The Book of Baruch | 104
   Summary | 109

Chapter 7: **CONCLUSION** | 111
   Summary of Chapters 2–6 | 111
   Exile: From Historical Event to Biblical Paradigm | 117

Bibliography | 119
Author Index | 131
Biblical Index | 135

ACKNOWLEDGEMENTS

I WANT TO THANK my Redemptorist confreres of the province of Oceania for giving me the opportunity and the necessary resources to research and write this book. I also wish to thank my confrere, Dr. Bruce Duncan CSSR (Yarra Theological Union), and colleagues Drs. Suzanne Boorer (Murdoch University) and Janina Hiebel (Yarra Theological Union) for reading earlier drafts of my manuscript and for their helpful comments and suggestions.

Thanks also to Cascade Books for accepting my manuscript for publication.

ABBREVIATIONS

AB	Anchor Bible
ABR	*Australian Biblical Review*
AfO	*Archiv für Orientforschung*
BBB	Bonner biblische Beiträge
BibInt	*Biblical Interpretation*
BibOr	Biblia et Orientalia
BIS	Biblical Interpretation Series
BKAT	Biblischer Kommentar, Altes Testament
BZAW	Beihefte zur Zeitschrift für die alttestamentliche Studien
BZNW	Beihefte zur Zeitschrift für die neutestamentliche Studien
CBQ	*Catholic Biblical Quarterly*
CRBR	*Critical Review of Books in Religion*
DSD	*Dead Sea Discoveries*
FAT	Forschungen zum Alten Testament
FRLANT	Forschungen zur Religion und Literatur des Alten und Neue Testaments
HTR	*Harvard Theological Review*
HUCA	*Hebrew Union College Annual*
ICC	International Critical Commentary
Int	*Interpretation*
JBL	*Journal of Biblical Literature*

ABBREVIATIONS

JETS	*Journal of the Evangelical Theological Society*
JHebS	*Journal of Hebrew Scriptures*
JSJ	*Journal for the Study of Judaism*
JSJSup	Journal for the Study of Judaism Supplements
JSOT	*Journal for the Study of the Old Testament*
JSOTSup	Journal for the Study of the Old Testament Supplements
JTS	*Journal of Theological Studies*
LHBOTS	The Library of Hebrew Bible/Old Testament Studies
LSTS	The Library of Second Temple Studies
NICOT	New International Commentary on the Old Testament
OBO	Orbis Biblicus et Orientalia
OBT	Overtures to Biblical Theology
OTL	Old Testament Library
OTS	Old Testament Studies
RB	*Revue biblique*
SBLABS	Society of Biblical Literature Archaeology and Biblical Studies
SBLDS	Society of Biblical Literature Dissertation Series
SBLEJL	Society of Biblical Literature Early Judaism and its Literature
SO	Symbolae Osloenses
STAR	Studies in Theology and Religion
VT	*Vetus Testamentum*
VTS	Vetus Testamentum Supplements
WBC	Word Biblical Commentary
WMANT	Wissenschaftliche Monographien zum Alten und Neuen Testament
WUNT	Wissenschaftliche Untersuchungen zum Neuen Testament
ZAW	*Zeitschrift für die alttestamentliche Wissenschaft*

Chapter 1

INTRODUCTION

When I googled the word "exile" I got about 148 million hits! Exile was a keyword for various thing such as a TV series, a band, a theme in music and literature. Most commonly however it referred to the experience of physical displacement, a fate of countless millions in our world today. If we live, as I do, in a country that was colonized by European powers in the last three hundred years or so, we live with indigenous peoples who have been forcibly moved off their land, and given few if any rights. In Australia, not only were our first peoples deprived of land, our federal constitution did not even recognize their existence until 1967. They became exiles in their own land. World Wars I and II, and the conflicts of this century too, created populations of exiles that numbered in the millions. No wonder the theme of exile has so permeated the arts and literature of so many cultures.

Exile is also a central theme of the Old Testament. A little over 2,500 years ago a small Middle Eastern country was invaded and conquered by a nearby superpower of the time. So, the Babylonian invasion of Judah and the forced displacement of some of its population was nothing to be wondered at. Right up until the recent past, human history has given us countless examples of large and powerful nations conquering smaller and less powerful ones. However, what is to be wondered at is how the effect of the events associated with 587 BCE have reverberated down through the ages. In the centuries that followed, the complex of events often referred to as the Babylonian exile, or just simply the exile, have been foundational in the development of both Second Temple Judaism and Christianity. The

Babylonian exile morphed from a series of historical events into a paradigm or an interpretive lens, which later generations would use to look at, and understand the events of their own era.

Studying the exile is not just about the past. The biblical texts reveal that, in today's world, we confront similar issues to those faced by the people of Israel in the aftermath of the Babylonian invasion. They had to come to grips with the collapse of their society and seeming impotence of their god. They searched for an explanation of why such a disaster happened. Those who were taken into exile had to make decisions about how to live in an alien culture, and to discern where their future lay. Those who survived the disaster and stayed in Judah had to contend with a different society, and struggled with issues about belonging to, and exclusion from, the community. These are familiar issues for the displaced and dispossessed of today. My aim in this book is to highlight these issues as I trace the development of the paradigm of exile.

In recent years there has been an explosion of literature on the Babylonian exile and its aftermath. So, why another book? The mountain of literature available means that for undergraduate students and non-specialist readers a study of the exile can be a daunting task.[1] So, my aim here is to make the extensive recent research on the exile more accessible, while acquainting readers with some of the newer approaches to the topic.

RECENT DEVELOPMENTS IN RESEARCH ON THE EXILE

Until relatively recently biblical scholars showed only a sporadic interest in the topic. This was due in part to the paucity of historical information available in the nineteenth century and most of the twentieth. Another factor was a prejudice about the state of Judaism in the Second Temple period. The situation began to change with the 1968 publication of the late Peter Ackroyd's magnificent study, *Exile and Restoration: A Study of Hebrew Thought in the Sixth Century BC*. In it he challenged a long-standing negative attitude of scholars to the Jewish religion, the belief that in the sixth century BCE and beyond, was in decline, was characterized by legalism, and lacked the inspiration of the great prophets and spiritual drive of earlier centuries. The subtitle of Ackroyd's work is an indication of his attitude: the period was a rich and creative era, as we have now come to realize.[2]

1. The literature is reviewed by Piotrowski, "The Concept of Exile."
2. Ackroyd, *Exile and Restoration*, 7–11. The importance and influence of this work

The early years of the current millennium saw the publication of new historical and archaeological data, which has given us a better picture of the sixth and fifth centuries BCE. In comparison to earlier periods such as the eighth century BCE and that of the Assyrian Empire, the data about the neo-Babylonian and early Persian periods is not as extensive. However, publications such as the Judah and the Judeans Series, edited by Oded Lipschits and others, have given us a better understanding than was previously possible.[3] We have become more aware of the impact of the exile on the development of the Hebrew Bible, and also on the New Testament's understanding of the mission of Jesus.[4]

The study of contemporary events in our world, such as the forced displacement of people and mass migration, have also contributed to the growth in studies of the Babylonian exile. Scholars have used insights from trauma and migration studies to better understand the effects of the Babylonian invasions of Judah and the forced displacement of its inhabitants. The collections of essays in *Interpreting Exile* and *The Prophets Speak on Forced Migration* provide good examples of the approach.[5]

---

was recognized in a collection of essays published after his death: Knoppers, Grabbe, and Fulton, *Exile and Restoration Revisited*.

3. The series includes: Lipschits and Blenkinsopp, *Judah and the Judeans in the Neo-Babylonian Period*; Lipschits and Oeming, *Judah and the Judeans in the Persian Period*; Lipschits, Knoppers, and Albertz, *Judah and the Judeans in the Fourth Century B.C.E.*; Lipschits, Knoppers, and Oeming, *Judah and the Judeans in the Achaemenid Period*. I also include here the developed and expanded version of Lipschits' doctoral dissertation, Lipschits, *The Fall and Rise of Jerusalem*.

4. On the Hebrew Bible see e.g., Ahn and Middlemas, *By the Irrigation Canals of Babylon*; Albertz and Becking, *Yahwism After the Exile*; Albertz, *Israel in Exile*; Ben Zvi and Levin, *Concept of Exile*; Berquist, *Approaching Yehud*; Scott, *Exile: Old Testament, Jewish and Christian Conceptions*; Stökl and Waerzeggers, *Exile and Return*.

On the Christian Scriptures, see especially N. T. Wright, *The New Testament and the People of God*. More recently, see Wright, *Yet the Sun Will Rise Again*, 19–22. His view about the centrality of the exile in the New Testament has been much discussed and scrutinized. On this see Scott, *Exile*.

5. See Kelle, Ames, and Wright, *Interpreting Exile*; Mark J. Boda et al., *The Prophets Speak on Forced Migration*. There are also important studies by John Ahn and Daniel Smith-Christopher: Ahn, *Exile as Forced Migrations*; Smith-Christopher, *Exile*.

EXILE AND RESTORATION?

The titles of Ackroyd's study, and the collection in his memory, raise a question about terminology, which we need to address here. The terms in question are "exile" and "restoration."

While the expression "the exile" can be a useful shorthand way of referring to the later years of the neo-Babylonian period, it can be misleading. Only a section of Judah's population was deported to Babylon, while others fled to neighboring countries in the face of the invasions, as well as in their aftermath. So, alongside of the community of exiles in Babylon and their descendants, there was the diaspora—literally, the scattering of people from Judah into other countries. Furthermore, biblical texts such as Lev 26:32–35 and 2 Chr 36:21 portray the land of Judah as totally empty of inhabitants after 587. As chapter 2 of this book will show, this portrait of an empty land is not historical. There was a forced migration of people from Judah to Babylon, but it did not involve the majority of Judah's population. So, to borrow the title of an essay by Philip Davies, we need to ask: "Exile? What Exile? Whose Exile?" Our study therefore is not just about the historical reconstruction of events in the sixth and fifth centuries BCE, but also includes how these events were interpreted, to what purpose, and by whom.

The exile of some Judahites to Babylon was not an isolated event, but happened in the context of the Babylonian conquest of Judah and the destruction of much of its infrastructure. So, when we consider the exile, we need to pay attention not only to the Babylonian conquest of Judah, but also to its impact on those who were not exiled. In the books of Jeremiah and Ezekiel, the threat of exile is often found along prophecies of invasion and destruction of the land. So, a study of exile includes a number of aspects. Besides the historical investigation of the neo-Babylonian conquest, there are the more obvious issues such as the fate of those deported to Babylon, the length of their exile, and their return to Judah. There is also the critical question of how the different biblical traditions interpreted the significance of the exile. It is clear then that in studying the exile, we are doing more than just looking at historical events. We are dealing with a construct, a series of events that has been overlaid with various levels of meaning.

Similarly, the term "restoration" is a construct, and a similar critique is needed for it. "Restoration" is used to refer to events that happened in the aftermath of the Persian conquest of Babylon.[6] It implies that "the exile" is

---

6. E.g., Foster, *The Restoration of Israel*; Japhet, *From the Rivers of Babylon*; Scott, *Restoration*.

over, and can be interpreted as saying that the society and institutions of pre-587 Judah have been put back in place. As we will see, there was no complete restoration of the society and institutions of the Judah that the Babylonians invaded, and no simple return to the homeland. So, again we need to ask: "whose restoration?" "what was restored?" and "whose point of view does this term represent?"

A further caution is also in order. In many texts exile is presented in completely negative terms. It is portrayed as a form of punishment by Yhwh for the sins of Judah. Its positive counterpart is restoration. The hope expressed in the biblical texts is that Yhwh will bring the exile to an end, and then lead those deported back to a rebuilt homeland, and a renewed relationship between them and him. While this understanding is very common, especially in the prophetic books of the time, we can also find another view, where those deported or their descendants make a home for themselves in the land of exile, and show no desire to journey back to the land of their ancestors.

OUTLINE OF THE BOOK

Chapter 2 is where our study begins. It looks at the historical events of the sixth century BCE in Syria-Palestine that gave rise to the Babylonian exile. There I investigate the invasions of Judah by the Babylonians under Nebuchadnezzar II, together with the destruction of infrastructure, and the subsequent deportations of a segment of its population. The chapter examines the critical questions of the number of people deported, the extent of the devastation caused by the Babylonians, and the nature of the society left in Judah after 587. The chapter sets the scene for what follows in chapter 3.

Chapter 3 is about responses to the disaster. Here we look at the book of Lamentations, with its outpouring of grief and confusion at what had happened. We also look at the explanations for the disaster found in the Deuteronomistic history and the books of Jeremiah and Ezekiel.

In chapter 4 the scene shifts from Judah to Babylon and the situation of the exiles there. We look at their living conditions, the challenges they faced as displaced people, and their visions of the future. The chapter describes the emergence of hope, and the process whereby the exiles and their descendants constructed a new identity suited to their changed situation. Here we read texts from Isa 40–55, the Priestly tradition, and the book of Ezekiel, and examine their respective visions about a future for the exiles.

In chapter 5 we enter a new phase, often referred to as the period of the restoration. Here we address the questions "did the exile end?" and "was there a restoration?" We look at the end of Babylonian domination, the rise of Persia, and what this meant for the community in Babylon, as well as for Judah and its inhabitants. The texts examined in chapter 5 are the book of Haggai and Zech 1–8, together with the books of Ezra and Nehemiah. As chapter 5 will show, in these texts there are ambiguities and different understandings about the end of the exile, as there are also with the idea of restoration. So, on the one hand, exile and exiles do not feature in Haggai. On the other hand, exile and exiles are central to the book of Ezra. What also becomes clear is that any rebuilding of Judah, its infrastructure and its institutions, was completely dependent on the goodwill of its new conqueror, the Persian overlords. So, while these events might constitute some form of restoration, there would be no renewed Judah, free from foreign control, and ruled by a Davidic monarch.

The ambiguity about the end of the exile and the attempts at restoration in chapter 5 give way in chapter 6 to a contrary view that the exile has not yet ended. In Isa 56–66 we see the sense of disillusionment and conflict in the community of Yehud, which gave rise to the belief that the future promised in Isa 40–55 had not materialized. In other words, the exile had not yet ended. There is also evidence of the same idea in the Hebrew recension of Jeremiah. The book begins and ends in exile. There are promises of a future, but these were yet to be realized. They were counterbalanced with threats of punishment and destruction, which were realized by the Babylonian conquest. Jeremiah MT situates its reader in exile. The book of Daniel, although the product of the second century BCE, situates its narratives and visions in the neo-Babylonian period. Daniel's community uses the image of the unended exile to make sense of the invasion of their land, and the desecration of the Jerusalem temple by their Seleucid occupiers.

Our study of exile concludes with chapter 7. It contains a summary of previous chapters, and puts forward some reflections about the current discussion of the place of exile in the Judaism of the early Common Era, and the Christian Gospels.

In the writing this book, I have proposed a particular way of understanding the development of exile as a biblical paradigm or metaphor.[7] In doing so, I have limited myself to considering only a certain number of

---

7. An example of another study, which uses a different set of texts, is the more technical one of Halvorson-Taylor, *Enduring Exile*.

texts. I have not examined texts such as the Psalms, the books of Chronicles, and Tobit, all of which reflect on the meaning of exile. My aim has been to present the topic so that a non-specialist student of the Bible can find their way through the extensive literature on the subject. I have tried to compose the book in such a way that it is possible to read it without referring to the footnotes (but not without a Bible!). I have used the footnotes to provide references at particular points so that interested readers can consult a broader range of literature, and the more specialized studies on specific issues related to the topic. Another use of the footnotes is to cite or discuss, where necessary, the meaning of various Hebrew or Greek words for readers familiar with the biblical languages.

Chapter 2

THE DISASTER OF 587 AND ITS AFTERMATH

IN THE EARLY SIXTH century BCE, the state of Judah was conquered by the Neo-Babylonian army of Nebuchadnezzar II, and incorporated into the administrative structure of the empire. As such, Judah ceased to exist. On the broad canvas of history, these events were nothing significant. A large and powerful empire invaded and appropriated a neighboring small state: a familiar story in human history, both ancient and modern. However, for Judah it was an event that totally undermined its whole identity. For some of its population, such as those who produced the book of Lamentations, the conquest made them wonder if Yhwh their God had totally abandoned them. Did the invasion and conquest mean the end of their nation and their religion?

In this chapter I will first set the scene by looking at pre-587 Judah and the foundations of its identity. This will help in understanding why the Babylonian conquest was such a crisis. Then I will take up the history of the Babylonian conquest in the early sixth century BCE.

SETTING THE SCENE: PRE-587 JUDAH

The foundation of pre-587 Judah as a society was a national theology.[1] It consisted of three core beliefs: the Jerusalem temple as the guarantee

---

1. The expression "national theology" goes back to Bright, *A History of Israel*, 311.

of Yhwh's presence and protection, continued rule by kings who were descendants of David, and the land as promised to Abraham. All three were regarded as divinely ordained.

The Jerusalem temple, built by Solomon, represented the presence of Yhwh with his people. With the temple came divine protection.[2] Portrayed as a woman and mother, Jerusalem was protected by her guardian-spouse, Yhwh, and so could not be conquered.[3] According to the theology, Yhwh had chosen Mt. Zion as his dwelling place.[4] Psalm 48:1–2 describes Jerusalem's unique status:

> Great is the LORD, and greatly to be praised in the city of our God.
> His holy mountain, beautiful in elevation, is the joy of all the earth.
> (vv. 1–2)

Defended by Yhwh it stands firm as its enemies attack in vain:

> Then the kings assembled, they came on together,
> As soon as they saw it, they were astounded;
> They were in panic; they took to flight. (vv. 4–5)

Belief in Jerusalem's immunity from attack was reinforced by the events of the year 701 BCE, when the Assyrian king Sennacherib surrounded the city and laid siege to it. At the height of the siege, and without any apparent reason, the Assyrians suddenly withdrew. Historians have speculated about the reasons for the withdrawal, but according 2 Kgs 18–20, the Assyrians withdrew because they were attacked by the angel of the LORD, who killed 185,000 of them. As a result, Jerusalem was safe, delivered by divine intervention, and in fulfillment of the promise made by Yhwh through the prophet Isaiah to King Hezekiah, that Sennacherib "would not come into this city ... for I will defend this city to save it" (2 Kgs 19:33–34). Under threat from the Babylonians 120 years later, the expectation was that the city, its king, and inhabitants, would all be similarly protected. As Jerusalem was under siege, king Zedekiah sent messengers to Jeremiah:

> Please inquire of the LORD on our behalf,
> for King Nebuchadrezzar of Babylon is making war against us;

---

2. For the background on the idea of Yhwh as Jerusalem's defender, see e.g., Maier, *Daughter Zion, Mother Zion*, 32–49; Ollenburger, *Zion, the City of the Great King*, 57–80.

3. On the feminine characterization of Jerusalem, see e.g., Maier, *Daughter Zion, Mother Zion*, 72–74.

4. The belief in mountains as the dwelling place of deities goes back to Canaanite mythology. For further, see Clements, *God and Temple*, 48–55.

> perhaps the LORD will perform his wonderful deeds for us,
> as he has often done, and will make him withdraw from us. (Jer 21:2)

"His wonderful deeds" is an allusion to the deliverance of Jerusalem in the time of Hezekiah. In 587 BCE, however, there would were no wondrous deeds, and no deliverance.

Another core belief was the continuation of the Davidic monarchy. Its validation by Yhwh is found in 2 Sam 7:1–17. Here the prophet Nathan receives an oracle, which he passes on to David. It promises that his descendants would be "established forever" (v. 16). The oracle allows for the possibility that any of David's descendants might do wrong, but, in that situation, Yhwh will punish but not disown or destroy the dynasty:

> I will be a father to him, and he shall be a son to me. When he commits iniquity, I will punish him with a rod such as mortals use, with blows inflicted by human beings.
> But I will not take my steadfast love from him, as I took it from Saul, whom I put away from before you. (vv. 14–15)

The oracle validates David's triumph over Saul and his accession to the kingship. It gives a divine, unconditional promise that Judah will always have a descendant of David as its king.

The promise of the land to Abraham, as expressed in Gen 12:1–9, was another foundational pillar of national identity. Abram is commanded by Yhwh to leave his homeland and travel to Canaan. There Yhwh appeared to him, and promised to give his descendants the land: "To your offspring I will give this land" (v. 7).[5] Pre-587 Judah saw itself as the descendants of Abraham, and so as the inheritors of a divinely guaranteed promise.

The invasions by the Babylonians, the subsequent destruction of infrastructure, and the deportations of some of Judah's inhabitants all need to be understood against the background of the national theology.

Another theological tradition existed alongside the Zion theology, one that originated with the Deuteronomistic theologians, who developed and redacted our present book of Deuteronomy. It had a different understanding about Judah's relationship with the land. The Deuteronomic tradition emphasized fidelity to the exclusive worship of Yhwh, and conceived of God's covenant with Israel as conditional. Infidelity would bring retribution

---

5. Gen 12:14a, 6–9, which contain the promise of land, come from the pre-Priestly stratum of Genesis (Boorer, *Vision*, 458–59).

in the form of banishment from the land.[6] However among the circles of power, such as the court and the temple, it lost out to the Zion theology.

CONQUEST, DISPOSSESSION, AND DEPORTATIONS— BIBLICAL ACCOUNTS

The Babylonians under Nebuchadnezzar II first invaded Judah and laid siege to Jerusalem in 597 BCE. The biblical descriptions of the city's siege and its aftermath are found in 2 Kgs 24:10–17. King Jehoiachin surrendered to the Babylonians, together with his family, his servants, court officials, and "the elite of the land" (v. 15).[7] They were deported to Babylon, along with soldiers and skilled workers (v. 16).[8] The Jerusalem temple and the king's residence were looted, and the spoils taken to Babylon. The biblical accounts also give the numbers of those deported, but these are difficult to interpret. According to 2 Kgs 24:14 there were also 10,000 captives taken to Babylon, whereas v. 16 refers to the deportation of 7,000. However, in Jer 52:28, the deportees are said to number "3,023 Judeans." Whatever we think about these differences, and how they might be accounted for, 2 Kgs 24:14 emphasizes the extent of the destruction and deportations:

> He [Nebuchadnezzar] carried away *all* Jerusalem, *all* the officials, *all* the warriors, ten thousand captives, *all* the artisans and the smiths; *no one remained*, except the poorest people of the land.[9]
> (2 Kgs 24:14)

The verse leaves us with a picture of a land reduced to ruins, with a small and insignificant population left behind.

In 587 BCE there was a second siege of Jerusalem by the Babylonian army. The biblical descriptions of the city's siege and its aftermath are found in 2 Kgs 25; Jer 39:1–10; and 52:4–30.[10] The royal family escaped during the siege but were then captured. King Zedekiah was taken to Babylon, where he was imprisoned until his death, but not before he had watched the

---

6. See, e.g., Mayes, *The Story of Israel between Settlement and Exile*; Ernest Nicholson, "Reconsidering the Provenance of Deuteronomy," 532–34.

7. Following the *Qere* of the MT: אילי הארץ ("leaders of the land").

8. Verse 16 refers to the deportation of גברים עשי מלחמה, which is translated in the NRSV as men "strong and fit for war."

9. Emphasis mine.

10. A briefer description of these events is found in 2 Chr 35:2–7.

execution of his sons (2 Kgs 25:5–7; Jer 39:1–7; 52:9–11). Nebuchadnezzar also burnt down the Jerusalem temple, the king's palace, all the houses in Jerusalem, and destroyed the city's walls. The temple was looted, and its metal fittings and furniture were removed and taken to Babylon (2 Kgs 25:9, 13–17; Jer 39:8; 52:13, 17–23).

As in 597, so in 587 there were deportations that again leave us with a picture of a land virtually empty of inhabitants:

> Nebuzaradan the captain of the guard carried into exile some of the poorest of the people and the rest of the people who were left in the city and the deserters who had defected to the king of Babylon, together with the rest of the artisans. But Nebuzaradan the captain of the guard left some of the poorest people of the land to be vinedressers and tillers of the soil. (2 Kgs 25:11–12; Jer 52:15–16; see also 39:10).

The end result, attested by both 2 Kgs 25:21 and Jer 52:27, is that "Judah went into exile out of its land."

The image of near to total desolation of Judah's land and society is also found Lev 18:24–25; 20:22; 26:34–43; Jer 24; 40–43; and 2 Chr 36:21. Leviticus 18:24–25 and 20:22 are part of the Holiness Code (chapters 18–26), and they portray the land as emptied out because of the sin of its inhabitants.[11] To this, Lev 26:34–43 adds the concept of the land as experiencing sabbath rest: "Then the land shall enjoy its sabbath years as long as it remains desolate" (v. 34).[12] The events of 587 and their aftermath are interpreted as fulfilling a prophecy of Jeremiah (Jer 25:11; 29:10) that the subjugation of Judah would last seventy years, during which time the land lies desolate, and keeps sabbath.[13]

The image of the empty land is also found in Jer 24, which describes a vision of the prophet followed by an explanation of its meaning. The vision is of two baskets of fruit—one edible and the other rotten. The former represents the deportees of 597 (v. 5), while the latter represents Zedekiah, together with those who remained in Judah after the disaster, and those who fled to Egypt (v. 8). The vision promises the deportees of 597 that they

---

11. A good summary of the central ideas of the Holiness Code is found in David P. Wright, "Holiness."

12. The reference to the sabbath rest is ambiguous in the Hebrew text. Verse 34 uses the verb רצה, which can mean "to enjoy," "take pleasure in" or "to repay." The imagery of Lev 18:24–25, and 26:34–43 is also found in 2 Chr 36:21.

13. 2 Chronicles 36:21 is a conflation of Lev 26:34 and Jeremian prophecies, that Judah's subjugation by Babylon would last seventy years (see Jer 25:12; 29:10).

will return to the land and occupy it. The inhabitants referred to in v. 8 will be completely exterminated, so that the deportees can return, and take possession of the land unhindered.

A different perspective on the idea of an empty land is also found in Jeremiah 40:7—42:13.[14] Unlike chapter 24, the land in Jer 40:7–13 has not been left empty in the aftermath of 587. Under Gedaliah, appointed by the Babylonians as a governor, a viable community of Judahites is established at Mizpah. The community existed until 582 when Gedaliah was assassinated by Judahite guerillas (41:1–3). Afraid of Babylonian retribution, the community's leaders intended to escape into Egypt, but decided to first consult Jeremiah about what they should do (42:1–3). His response was that they should stay in the land, and Yhwh would keep them safe. To escape into Egypt would lead to disaster: "If you are determined to enter Egypt and go to settle there, the sword will overtake you . . . and there you shall die" (v. 6). Death would not be the fate of the leaders only, but of all the community who go to Egypt: "They shall have no remnant or survivor from the disaster I [Yhwh] am bringing on them" (v. 17). Despite the prophet's warning, the leaders took all the community down to Egypt, and left behind an empty land.

The representation of an empty, desolate land does not reflect the historical reality of post-587 Judah, but is rather an ideological or theological construction. Its significance is disputed by scholars. Some say it serves to advance the land claims of particular groups in the period after the end of Babylonian domination.[15] In 2 Chr 36:20, the seventy years of Judah's subjugation comes to an end with the rise of Cyrus, and the ascendency of the Persians. The land now stands empty, waiting to be repopulated by the returning exiles from Babylon (2 Chr 36:22–23; Ezra 1). Similarly, in Jeremiah 24 the exiles of 597 are promised that they will return and take possession of a desolate, empty land.

Other scholars relate the idea of the empty land to an understanding of Yhwh's punitive action in the events surrounding 587.[16] Prophets like Jeremiah and Ezekiel had announced that Judah's sinful behavior would bring down divine punishment on the land. The Babylonian conquest was the expression of Yhwh's anger. Not only was there the suffering of invasion,

---

14. Stipp, "Empty Land."

15. For this view see, e.g. Carroll, "The Myth of the Empty Land"; Barstad, "The Myth of the Empty Land."

16. E.g Ben Zvi, "Total Exile."

death, and destruction, but there was also Yhwh's withdrawal from the Jerusalem temple, which had become defiled by the actions of its worshipers (Ezek 8–11). For there to be any kind of future for the people, there had to be a complete separation between the old era and the new. The land, polluted by the sins of its inhabitants, must now remain empty, until a time in the future when Yhwh will allow it to be populated again. As the biblical texts show, 587 is remembered as a ground-zero moment, which called into question the very foundations of Judah's identity as a community whose survival was supposed to be divinely guaranteed.

POST-587 JUDAH

To get a clearer understanding of the state of Judah after the conquest, we need to reckon not only with the biblical accounts, but also with data from archeological and other sources. In the light of current debates about post-587 Judah, and the state of its infrastructure, we need to realize that the amount of historical and archaeological material from this period is relatively small, especially when compared to discoveries from the Neo-Assyrian period.[17] So, positions taken here must be regarded as probable, rather than certain.[18] I will now take up two aspects of life in the aftermath of the

17. As pointed out by Faust, *Judah in the Neo-Babylonian Period*, 149–66; Vanderhooft, "Babylonian Strategies," 235–42.

18. At present there are sharply divided opinions about the historical validity of the biblical accounts of the Babylonian invasion and its aftermath. The traditional view, put forward by scholars such as William Albright and John Bright accepts the biblical accounts of a devastated society as substantially historical, apart from the representation of the land as totally empty, and devoid of inhabitants:

> Though the popular notion of a total deportation which left the land empty and void is erroneous and to be discarded, the catastrophe was nevertheless appalling and one which signaled the disruption of Jewish life in Palestine. (Bright, *A History of Israel*, 343–44)

The extensive nature of the damage is argued emphatically by Albright, *Archaeology*, 140–42.

Today supporters of the traditional view refer to post-587 Judah as a "post-collapse society," and emphasize the substantial difference between pre-587 Judah and the society that emerged as Yehud in the Persian period (Faust, *Judah in the Neo-Babylonian Period*, 168–76; Vanderhooft, "Babylonian Strategies"; Stern, "The Babylonian Gap"). According the supporters of this view, it is critical to understand that a post-collapse society, such as post-587 Judah, suffered not only a severe loss in population and infrastructure, but that this happened both quickly and traumatically, and not over an extended period of time.

Babylonian conquest. The first issue to examine is the depopulation of Judah and Jerusalem; the second the destruction of land and infrastructure.[19]

At the end of the Iron Age (seventh century BCE), Judah's population was estimated by scholars to have been between 110,000 and 140,000.[20] In the early Persian period, it is estimated at 30,000.[21] We need to keep in mind that a number of factors could lead to depopulation, such as death in battle, death of non-combatants, starvation during sieges, people fleeing from Judah as refugees, as well as the Babylonian forced deportations of the local population. On this basis, it is estimated that between 600 and 580 Judah lost 30 percent, 50 percent, or even 80 percent of its population.[22]

The other aspect of post-587 Judah to consider is the destruction of its infrastructure. The levels of destruction varied from place to place, and there is disagreement among scholars about their significance. There is general agreement that there was extensive destruction in Jerusalem in the sixth century: in the City of David, the Ophel, the citadel, and the area that corresponds to the modern Jewish Quarter.[23] The temple was either sub-

---

These scholars are reacting to an approach that argues that the biblical descriptions of extreme disaster are exaggerated, and that "life went on after 586 pretty much in the same way that it did before the arrival of Nebuchadnezzar's armies" (Barstad, "Major Challenges," 14; see also Carroll, "The Myth of the Empty Land"; Barstad, "The Myth of the Empty Land"; Blenkinsopp, "The Bible, Archaeology and Politics"). This approach has been labelled "the continuity theory" (Faust, *Judah in the Neo-Babylonian Period*, 181).

19. The sometimes sharp disagreements between the advocates of the two approaches outlined above have various causes. In some cases, their conclusions are different because they are referring to different archaeological sites. In other cases, there is disagreement as to which archaeological period an artefact belongs. Also, the significance or importance of particular artefacts may have been evaluated differently. Then there are the two different attitudes to the historicity of the biblical accounts. Is the biblical record influencing the archaeological conclusions, or is the biblical record to be treated with skepticism? Also, at times, the contemporary conflict between the land claims of Israel and the Palestinians intrudes into the debate (e.g Blenkinsopp, "The Bible, Archaeology and Politics"). A final observation is that the use of polemical labels also intrudes into the discussion. So, Faust accuses the advocates of the continuity theory of constructing a "straw man" by their portrait of the empty land, while Lipschits refers to the former's views as "extreme" and "ultra-conservative" (Faust, *Judah in the Neo-Babylonian Period*, 185; Lipschits, "Shedding New Light," 84 n.101).

20. For a detailed treatment see Lipschits, "Demographic Changes."

21. Lipschits, "Demographic Changes," 364. His figure of 30,000 is regarded as too high by Faust, who however does not suggest an alternative (Faust, *Judah in the Neo-Babylonian Period*, 129).

22. Albertz, *Israel in Exile*, 89–90; Faust, *Judah in the Neo-Babylonian Period*, 169.

23. Lipschits, "Demographic Changes," 328.

stantially or totally destroyed, and Jerusalem lost most of its inhabitants. Its settled area was diminished by nearly 90 percent.[24] It lay mostly in ruins until well into the Persian period, and did not become the capital city again until the middle of the fifth century.[25]

Although there was extensive devastation of some rural areas, others escaped more lightly. Areas such as the Jordan valley and the Shephelah, an area in western Judahite highlands, were severely damaged, and lost two-thirds or more of their settled areas.[26] The area south of Jerusalem around Ramat Raḥel fared better, as did the territory of Benjamin, which however still saw the destruction of up to one third of its settled areas.[27] After 587, the administrative center of Judah moved to Mizpah. Here Gedaliah acted as the Babylonian overlord until his assassination in 582. The site continued to be occupied, and functioned as an administrative center down into the fifth century.[28] The exact nature of the Babylonian presence in post-587 Judah is not known. There may have been some military installations to guard the empire's borders against the Egyptians, but their size and locations are not clear. This is also true about the presence of any Babylonian administrative officials.[29]

However uncertain our knowledge of post-587 Judah may be, it is certain that the Babylonian conquest was a major trauma, because it called into question not only Judah's identity and foundations, but also because it raised the possibility that Judah's existence as a society and a nation had come to an end.

---

24. Lipschits, "Demographic Changes," 356.
25. Lipschits, "Achaemenid Imperial Policy," 30–40.
26. Lipschits, "Demographic Changes," 338–46.
27. On Ramat Raḥel, see Lipschits, "Shedding New Light," 58–66. On the destruction of Benjamin, see Lipschits, "Demographic Changes," 363.
28. On the archaeology of Mizpah, see Zorn, "Tell en-Naṣbeh." For a more skeptical view, see Vanderhooft, "Babylonian Strategies," 254–55; Betylon, "Neo-Babylonians Military Operations," 268–72.
29. "Too little evidence exists to support the claim that the Babylonians installed an effective imperial administration in these regions during Nebuchadnezzar's reign" (Vanderhooft, "Babylonian Strategies," 235). For a different view, see Sack, "Nebuchadnezzar II," 226–30.

SUMMARY

The Babylonian invasion and its aftermath left behind a devastated country. Examination of biblical texts and archaeological data has allowed us to understand something of the extent of Judah's devastation. Jerusalem, its capital and religious center, was substantially destroyed, possibly to the extent where the city was uninhabitable. Its temple was wrecked and desecrated. Much of the Judahite countryside was also destroyed, with the exception of Benjamin, and a small area south of Jerusalem around Ramat Raḥ. After 587 the administrative center of Judah was moved to Mizpah, which continued to function in this role down into the fifth century.

While Judah was not left an empty land, as some of the biblical texts suggest, it still suffered a substantial loss of its population, estimated to be as high as 80 percent. Members of the royal family, palace and temple officials, and artisans were deported to Babylon. They comprised the leadership and educated classes of the society. The majority of the population were not deported but were left to survive in a devastated society. (So it is evident that the non-exiled population was massively depleted by other factors, such as flight from a devastated land and death from a range of causes.)

Because the disasters of 597, 587, and 592 signified the collapse of the national theology, the devastation was not just material. Those who survived, both those who stayed in the land and those who were deported, faced *a theological crisis*. Was Yhwh impotent in the face of the Babylonian deities? Or had he abandoned his people altogether? What sort of future awaited the people in Judah? These questions are for the next chapter.

Chapter 3

RESPONSES TO THE DISASTER
Grief and Explanations

DISASTERS RAISE ALL SORTS of questions for survivors. Often the most pressing is "why?" A disaster like that of 587 raised critical questions for its survivors. Did the conquest mean that Yhwh was impotent in the face of the Babylonian deities? Was the conquest an expression of Yhwh's anger and displeasure at the people of Judah? Did Yhwh then decide to abandon them? In this chapter we look at two kinds of responses to the disaster. One was an outpouring of grief, found in the book of Lamentations. The other was a search for explanations, found in the Deuteronomistic History and the books of Jeremiah and Ezekiel.

GRIEF AND THE BOOK OF LAMENTATIONS

The Babylonian invasions and final conquest of Judah was a theological trauma, which the community struggled to understand. The profound grief that accompanied it was movingly expressed in the book of Lamentations.

The book of Lamentations consists of five chapters, each of which is a poem, containing expressions of grief and confusion about the destruction of Jerusalem. In this context the city is a metonymy for Judah and its people as a whole. The book ends with an unresolved tension: in the light of the Babylonian conquest, is this the end of Judah, its people, and its relationship with Yhwh?

In order to appreciate the significance of its conclusion, we need to briefly read through the book from its beginning. Its first four chapters were composed in acrostic form—i.e., the first verse starts with the first letter of the Hebrew alphabet, the second verse with the second letter, and so on, until the last verse, which begins with the last letter of the alphabet. There are twenty-two letters in the Hebrew alphabet, and so there are twenty-two verses in chapters 1, 2, and 4. In chapter 3 there are sixty-six verses in a variation of the acrostic pattern, and in chapter 5 the pattern is absent. The effect of the acrostic pattern in chapters 1, 2 and 4 is to provide an orderly way of describing what is chaotic and shambolic, i.e., the destruction of Jerusalem, and the grief which accompanied it.[1] The significance of the different patterns found in chapters 3 and 5 will be explained below.

Lamentations 1–4

Chapter 1 divides into two sections: the voice of the narrator (vv. 1–11b) and the voice of Jerusalem (vv. 11c–22).[2] It is dominated by themes of "shame, mourning and suffering."[3] The theme of shame is found in the portrait of Jerusalem as a woman abandoned by her lovers, stripped naked for everyone to see, and assaulted by those who once were her friends (vv. 2, 5, 8).[4] The theme of mourning runs right through the chapter. In vv. 1–11b the narrator describes the mourning of Jerusalem, and then in vv. 11c–22 we hear Jerusalem herself. In vv. 12, 20–22 she calls out so that Yhwh might see her suffering and distress: "O Lord, look at my affliction . . ." (v. 12), "See, o Lord, how distressed I am" (v. 22). She also calls out to those passing by to "look and to see if there any sorrow like my sorrow" (v. 12). Chapter 1 makes clear the reason for her devastation, both in the persona of the narrator and of Jerusalem herself. In v. 5 the narrator declares that her suffering is because of "the multitude of her transgressions," and that

---

1. "The strict acrostic form is designed so that the reader, deeply moved by the dreadful situations described in the book, will return to it for a second reading, but this time in order to reflect on it. In order for the laments to be read as a book that conveys a message, the author created an intentional tension between form and content—between the unrestrained content and the restricted form" (Assis, "Alphabetic Acrostic," 716).

2. Following O'Connor, *Lamentations*, 23.

3. Berlin, *Lamentations*, 47.

4. In the ancient world, a city was often portrayed as a woman protected by a male deity. For a fuller treatment, see Berlin, *Lamentations*, 7–12; Dobbs-Allsopp, *Weep, O Daughter of Zion*; Berlin, *Lamentations*, 7–12; Galambush, *Jerusalem*, 20–25.

she has "sinned grievously" (v. 7). Jerusalem herself admits her guilt (vv. 14, 19), and admits that Yhwh's punishment of her is justified: "The LORD is in the right, for I have rebelled against his word" (v. 18).

Chapter 1 ends with Jerusalem calling on Yhwh to take her side, and to do to her enemies what Yhwh has done to her. She imagines them as gloating over her downfall (v. 21) and so appeals for retribution (vv. 21–22). The chapter begins with the description of Jerusalem as lonely and abandoned like a widow (v. 1), and ends in a similar way. Filled with anguish and looking for comfort, Jerusalem calls out, but there is no response. Yhwh does not see or answer. She remains abandoned.[5]

Chapter 2 consists of two sections. In vv. 1–10, 11–19, the narrator speaks. In vv. 20–22 Jerusalem pleads with Yhwh.[6] The chapter uses progressively more intense language to describe the destruction of Jerusalem. It emphasizes not only that the destruction has been brought about by Yhwh himself, but that it had even been planned long ago: "As he planned long ago, he has demolished without pity" (v. 17). In vv. 1–10, there is a string of verbs related to the idea of destruction, and these all have Yhwh as the subject: e.g., humiliate, throw down (v. 1), destroy, break (v. 2), burn (v. 3), abolish (v. 6) etc. The cumulative effect of these verbs is to characterize Yhwh as a punitive and destructive deity.[7] It is as if in anger Yhwh has turned against himself:

> He has broken down *his* booth . . .
> He has destroyed *his* tabernacle . . .
> The LORD has scorned *his* altar, disowned *his* sanctuary . . . (2:6)

Instead of being the lover and protector of Jerusalem, Yhwh has now become its enemy and destroyer (v. 5).

In vv. 11–19 the third person speech of vv. 1–10 gives way now to first person speech, in which the narrator grieves and weeps for Jerusalem. Verse 15 quotes from Ps 48, a text that is an expression of the Zion theology, and its elevated understanding of Jerusalem as divinely protected against any enemy. Lamentations 1:15 reads:

> All who pass by clap their hands at you;
> they hiss and wag their heads at daughter Jerusalem;

---

5. On Yhwh's silence, see Boase, "Characterisation of God," 37; Harris and Mandolfo, "The Silent God in Lamentations."

6. So Berlin, *Lamentations*, 67.

7. Boase, "Characterisation of God," 35.

RESPONSES TO THE DISASTER

"Is this the city that was called the perfection of beauty,
the joy of all the earth?" (1:15)

Verse 15 refers to Ps 48, which portrays Jerusalem standing firm against its assailants who are reduced to a panic-stricken rabble. Psalm 48:1–2 describes Jerusalem's unique status:

> Great is the LORD, and greatly to be praised in the city of our God.
> His holy mountain, beautiful in elevation, is the joy of all the earth." (vv. 1–2)

Defended by Yhwh it stands firm as its enemies attack in vain:

> Then the kings assembled, they came on together,
> As soon as they saw it, they were astounded;
> They were in panic; they took to flight. (vv. 4–5)

The destruction of Jerusalem then turns this theology on its head. Not only is Jerusalem crushed and conquered, the triumphant enemy is *Yhwh himself*, the city's supposed protector.[8] It is for this reason that the devastation of Jerusalem is so incomprehensible: what has become of Yhwh her protector? Like the previous chapter, Lam 2 closes with an unanswered plea that Yhwh might look and attend to Jerusalem's pain (Lam 2:20).

In chapter 3 there is a change in the acrostic pattern. It has sixty-six verses, instead of twenty-two. Each verse consists of only one line of poetry. The acrostic pattern is reflected in the chapter's structure, whereby the first three verses begin with the first letter of the Hebrew alphabet (labeled as v. 1 in our Bibles), the second three verses with the second letter (all grouped as v. 2 in our Bibles), the third three verses with the third letter (grouped into v. 3), and so on. The last three verses (v. 22) begin with the last letter of the Hebrew alphabet. Compared to chapters 1 and 2, the structure of chapter 3 is much tighter, giving a controlled way for the speaker to describe in detail his terrible sufferings. Where the imagery in chapter 1 is feminine,

---

8. The failure of the Zion theology is also evident in the book of Jeremiah, especially in chapter 1. Here Yhwh will establish Jeremiah as a fortified city (v. 18), while Jerusalem faces destruction. The imagery of foreign invaders at the gates of Jerusalem recalls the Zion traditions, among which is the theme of the *Völkerkampf*—the assault of the foreign nations on the divinely protected Jerusalem. However, where in Ps 48 Yhwh is the defender of the city (v. 4; v. 3 NRSV), in Jer 1:15 he is responsible for the attack. This attack by Yhwh against Jerusalem means that Jerusalem is no longer the city of Yhwh protected by his power. The theology of the Zion's divine protection has completely collapsed. For further discussion, see Carroll, *Jeremiah*, 106–7; Nasuti, "A Prophet to the Nations: Diachronic and Synchronic Readings of Jeremiah 1," 256–57.

in chapter 3 it is masculine and reflects the language of war. The speaker is a man. His identity is not clear, except that he is someone who knows the pain and suffering of a defeated warrior.[9]

Absent to this point in the book, the theme of hope appears in chapter 3, which can be broadly divided into two sections: vv. 1–42 speak about Yhwh in the third person, and vv. 43–66 address him directly.

Verses 1–42 contain a description of distress (vv. 1–21), followed by a confession of trust in Yhwh (vv. 22–42). Verses 1–21 describe the experience of being under the wrath of Yhwh. In language similar to that in the book of Job, the speaker describes the physical punishment and distress inflicted on him by Yhwh (vv. 1–13), the abuse heaped on him by his own people (vv. 14–16), and the sadness of being abandoned by Yhwh (vv. 17–20).[10] However, in v. 21 a change occurs. For the first time in the book, there is a hope. Painful as his suffering has been, the speaker sees in it a reason to hope: "But this I call to mind, and therefore I have hope." Verses 22–42 contain his confession of trust in Yhwh, and a recognition of his justice. The speaker puts his trust in the "steadfast love," the "mercies," and the "faithfulness" of Yhwh (vv. 22–23), qualities that in Exod 34:6 Yhwh uses to describe himself.[11]

In v. 42b there is a shift from talking about Yhwh to addressing him directly, and this continues until the end of the chapter (v. 66). Verses 43–54 contain another outpouring of grief, followed by a confession of trust in Yhwh (vv. 55–63), and an invocation that Yhwh will avenge the suffering of the speaker (vv. 64–66). As in the earlier part of the chapter, the theme of hope appears again, as the speaker calls to mind an intervention of Yhwh in the past. However, vv. 64–66 brings the reader back to the unresolved pain and grief of the present. The call for vengeance in vv. 64–66 against Jerusalem's enemies is incongruous, because earlier parts of the chapter 3 indicate that Jerusalem's enemy is actually Yhwh. It is as if the speaker is now oblivious to how he spoke earlier. Chapter 3 ends in the same way as chapters 1 and 2, with a plea to Yhwh to look that remains unanswered.

Chapter 3, the longest poem in the book, is now followed by the much shorter chapter 4. It has twenty-two verses, as do chapters 1 and 2, but

---

9. In the past it was thought to be a historical figure, like a Jeremiah. More recently scholars have suggested it might be a defeated warrior, or a collective group. For these suggestions, see Berlin, *Lamentations*, 84.

10. On the similarities with the book of Job, see Berlin, *Lamentations*, 85, 92–93.

11. So, Berlin, *Lamentations*, 93; Westermann, *Lamentations*, 173.

where they have three lines of poetry, chapter 4 has two. Its theme has been summed up as "degradation" or "diminishment."[12] Two voices speak in the chapter, an anonymous narrator (vv. 1–16) and the people of Jerusalem (vv. 17–22). In vv. 1–10 the narrator describes the appalling suffering of the inhabitants of a city under siege: children starving (v. 4), people eating from the garbage dumps (v. 5), and desperate enough to resort to cannibalism (v. 10).[13] Verses 11–16 offer a theological reflection on the disaster. The wrath of Yhwh has brought it about, and the narrator lays the blame at the feet of the prophets and priests (v. 13). Although he acknowledges that Yhwh brought about the destruction, he is still caught up in the Zion theology, and still struggles to come to terms with what has happened:

> The kings of the earth did not believe,
> nor did any of the inhabitants of the world,
> that foe or enemy could enter the gates of Jerusalem. (3:12)

In reality "the kings of the earth" and "the inhabitants of the world" could not have cared less about what happened to an insignificant city like Jerusalem. But it was the believer in the Zion theology who could not comprehend what had happened, and who struggled with the possibility that Yhwh had abandoned Jerusalem.

In vv. 17–20 the people express grief and disappointment, especially about the fate of their king, "the LORD's anointed" (v. 20). The ruler in question is generally regarded as Zedekiah, the Davidic king whom the Babylonians appointed instead of Jehoiachin after the siege of 597.[14] Again, their attachment to the Zion theology makes more difficult their comprehension of the disaster and its causes, as they believed that the rule of a Davidic king would have protected them. In reference to his role, they say "Under his shadow we shall live among the nations" (v. 20). In chapter 4 there is a desolation (vv. 1–11), a recognition of Yhwh's punishment, together with the reasons for it (vv. 11, 13), and an inability to grasp its significance because of the people's attachment to the Zion theology. Then, like chapters 1, 2 and 3, chapter 4 ends with the hope of retribution (vv. 21–22).

---

12. "Degradation" is the term used by Berlin, *Lamentations*, 98; "diminishment" comes from O'Connor, *Lamentations*, 58.

13. Verse 5b in the NRSV describes people as clinging "to ash heaps," but Berlin gives a much more graphic translation: "those reared in crimson huddled in garbage dumps" (Berlin, *Lamentations*, 99).

14. Berlin, *Lamentations*, 113.

Lamentations 5

Chapter 5 concludes the book. It has twenty-two verses, which consist of only one line, making them the shortest of any in the whole book. It also lacks the acrostic pattern. The chapter gives a summary of the sufferings of Jerusalem. There is the loss of land and family life (v. 2–3), the lack of food and water (vv. 4–10), the sufferings of those defeated in war (v. 11–13), and the desolate state of the city (vv. 14–18). The chapter begins and ends with an invocation to Yhwh to remember and not forget Jerusalem's distress (vv. 1, 20), and a call for him to restore and renew his relationship with her (v. 21). It has some of the characteristics of a psalm of lament. Verse 1 is an invocation of Yhwh, vv. 2–18 is the description of the distress, v. 19 is the expression of trust or confidence in Yhwh, and vv. 20–22 is the petition for him to intervene.[15]

As in Lam 1, the question of responsibility for the disaster occurs also in chapter 5. There are two references, and they stand in tension with each other. According to 5:7 the cause of Judah's downfall is the sin of the ancestors, but it is the descendants who suffer the consequences. But in 5:16, the disaster is the fault of the present generation: "Woe to us, for we have sinned." There are two ways to explain the tension. One is that the present generation are calling into question the link between sin and punishment, and implying that they are being unfairly punished for something they did not do.[16] A more commonly accepted interpretation is that the responsibility belongs both to the ancestors and the present generation. It is a question of a guilt that has accumulated over the generations. Both the ancestors and the present generation are equally guilty.[17] The tension in the text may simply reflect the community's confusion and sense of ambiguity about the disaster and its causes: somebody must have sinned for it to have happened, but was it us or our ancestors?

Ambiguity and confusion also surround the final verses of the book (vv. 20–22), which go the heart of the theology. Formally they resemble the

---

15. Westermann, *Lamentations*, 211. Chapter 5 differs from the usual lament genre with its long complaint section (vv. 2–18), its short statement of confidence in Yhwh (v. 19), and the absence of a vow of praise (Williamson Jr., "Lamentations 5," 73).

For an extensive explanation of the structure of the lament psalm, see Westermann, *Praise and Lament in the Psalms*, 165–213.

16. This argument is developed at length by Wagner, "Die Schuld."

17. Bier, *Reading Lamentations*, 171; Renkema, *Lamentations*, 606, 618–19; Westermann, *Lamentations*, 215. For a different approach, see Berlin, *Lamentations*, 120–21.

petition for Yhwh's intervention, as in a communal lament, but come with a sting in the tail:

> Why have you forgotten us completely?
> Why have you forsaken us these many days?
> Restore us to yourself, O LORD, that we may be restored;
> renew our days as of old
> unless you have utterly rejected us,
> and are angry with us beyond measure . . . . (5:20–22)

Verse 20 contains language that is common in laments, especially references to Yhwh's "forgetting" and "forsaking" his people. The tense of these verbs in Hebrew indicates that Yhwh's forgetting and forsaking did not happen just with the events of 587, but that he continued to abandon his people.[18] Verse 22 gives Lamentations a very distinctive ending, or non-ending—an unresolved doubt about Yhwh's intentions. The last line in the book does not provide any resolution of Jerusalem's fate or future, but trails off into an inconclusive and unfinished possibility.[19] The absence of the acrostic pattern points to the confusion and grief suffered by the community, and to its disintegration. Where, earlier in the book, the acrostic pattern helped to give some shape and order to the community's expressions of grief, its absence in chapter 5 indicates that ultimately the community can find no meaning in the chaos of the collapse that surrounded it. It calls on Yhwh, but there is no response. His refusal to answer leaves the community facing the possibility that their existence and their relationship with him may be at an end.[20]

---

18. The verbs "forgotten" (שכח) and "forsaken" (עזב) in the MT of v. 20 are both in the imperfect tense. "The question put to Yahweh is not simply why did you forget/abandon us when the Babylonians besieged and then destroyed our cities, our Temple, our lives, but why do you continue to do so?" (Salters, *Lamentations*, 370).

19. The unresolved nature of the verse is highlighted by Linafelt's translation, which leaves the last verse unfinished: "if you truly have rejected us, raging bitterly against us —" (Linafelt, "Refusal," 343). For Berlin, the concluding chapter and "the book as a whole fail to provide the comfort that has been sought throughout it" (Berlin, *Lamentations*, 125). For a summary of the translations advocated by the various English versions and scholars, see Nguyen, *Chorus in the Dark*, 201–3; Parry, *Lamentations*, 154–57; Renkema, *Lamentations*, 631.

20. "Lamentations is a plea for comfort in the form of access to God. The plea throughout the book is that God should hear, see, remember, pay attention, and, at its climax, that he should 'take us back' (5:21), but the plea is never answered, God remains silent, and so in this book, the state of mourning cannot end" (Berlin, "On Writing a Commentary on Lamentations," 9).

EXPLANATIONS OF THE DISASTER

While Lamentations expressed the grief and confusion felt by the community, there was a need for something further—explanations of why the disaster occurred. These were provided by the Deuteronomistic History, and the books of Jeremiah and Ezekiel.

The Deuteronomistic History

The Deuteronomists attributed responsibility for the disaster firstly to Judah's kings, and subsequently to the whole nation. Before examining their interpretation, we need to clarify what the Deuteronomistic History is, and who were its creators.

The Deuteronomistic History, prefaced by Deuteronomy, extends from the book of Joshua to 2 Kings. The Deuteronomistic History (Dtrh) hypothesis is that these books present an interpretation of Israel's history that is the result of a systematic redaction.[21] The composers of the history are anonymous, and are referred to as Deuteronomists. They are said to belong to the Deuteronomistic tradition, school, or movement. The history comprises what in the Hebrew Bible are consecutive books: Joshua, Judges, 1 and 2 Samuel, 1 and 2 Kings. It presents a theological interpretation of the history of Israel and Judah from the time of Moses until the Babylonian conquest. This circle of composers and redactors are called Deuteronomists because they drew their inspiration from the book of Deuteronomy, with its emphasis on the exclusive worship of the one God, Yhwh.

The first edition of the history appeared during the reign of Josiah, and "was composed principally as a history of Israel's leaders."[22] It provided a report card on the reign of each of the kings of Israel and Judah. Apart from David, Hezekiah, and Josiah, the evaluations of the kings were predominantly negative because they engaged in syncretistic worship on the high places. The first edition of the history vindicated Josiah's expansion of Judah's borders to the north, and his centralization of worship in the

---

21. For an introduction to the scholarship about the Deuteronomistic History hypothesis, see e.g., Albertz, *Israel in Exile*, 271–85 Campbell and O'Brien, *Deuteronomistic History*, 11–13; Nelson, "The Double Redaction"; Römer and de Pury, "Deuteronomistic Historiography (DH)."

22. O'Brien, *The Deuteronomistic History Hypothesis: A Reassessment*, 27. See also Campbell and O'Brien, *Deuteronomistic History*, 20–22; Römer, *The So-Called Deuteronomistic History*, 97–106; Cross, *Canaanite Myth and Hebrew Epic*.

Jerusalem temple. His fidelity to the Deuteronomic theology of exclusive worship of Yhwh was seen as overriding the infidelity of the earlier kings. It also celebrated his status as the most faithful of Judah and Israel's kings: "Before him there was no king like him, who turned to the LORD" (2 Kgs 23:25). However, his untimely death in 609 and then the Babylonian conquests in 597 and 587 needed explanations, and so the history was updated.

After describing the conquest of Jerusalem in 587, this first exilic addition concluded with the notice, "So Judah went into exile out of its land" (2 Kgs 25:21).[23] The edition laid the blame for the disaster squarely on the shoulders of the kings.[24] In the Josianic edition of the history, the collective evil of the kings was cancelled out by Josiah's fidelity. In the exilic edition, the figure of Manasseh, who ruled Judah from around 687 to 642 BCE, becomes a special focus for the Deuteronomistic redactors.[25] Already portrayed negatively in the Josianic edition for his syncretistic worship (2 Kgs 21:2a, 3, 5, 7), he is now said to have engaged in child sacrifice and consulted wizards and mediums (v. 6). Because of Manasseh's evil, Yhwh will destroy Jerusalem and its inhabitants (21:10-14). Also his evil was so great, it cancelled out all the good that Josiah did. Great as Josiah was, Yhwh's anger "was kindled against Judah because of all the provocations with which Manasseh had provoked him [i.e., Yhwh]" (23:26). His responsibility for the disasters then is reaffirmed in the history's account of Nebuchadnezzar's conquest of Jerusalem in 597 BCE: "Surely this came upon Judah at the command of the LORD, to remove them out of his sight for the sins of Manasseh, for all that he had committed..." (24:3).[26]

The Book of Jeremiah: "You Defiled My Land"

In the book of Jeremiah responsibility belongs to everyone, both rulers and the community at large. The whole nation is accused of worshiping deities

---

23. See Campbell and O'Brien, *Deuteronomistic History*, 470.

24. Campbell and O'Brien, *Deuteronomistic History*, 19-20; Römer, *The So-Called Deuteronomistic History*, 157-58.

25. For further on Manasseh, see Halpern, "Why Manasseh Is Blamed"; Römer, *The So-Called Deuteronomistic History*, 159-61; O'Brien, *The Deuteronomistic History Hypothesis: A Reassessment*, 227-34.

26. For further on the provenance of 2 Kgs 24:2-4, see. Campbell and O'Brien, *Deuteronomistic History*, 467 n.108.

other than Yhwh, of rejecting Jeremiah's calls to repentance, and ignoring his proclamations of impending judgment.

Chapters 2–6 interpret the people's history in the land as one of infidelity, in contrast to the time in the wilderness, which was characterized by innocence and fidelity to Yhwh (2:2–3). In Jer 2:3 Israel is said to be "holy to the LORD, the first fruits of his harvest." According to Deut 26:9, they belong to him alone.[27] The vision of Israel's fidelity in 2:2–3 stands in stark contrast to their behavior in the land, which Jer 2–6 characterizes as one of infidelity and sin. The Jeremiah tradition has an ironical view of the people's history. Their fidelity in the desert turned a place of death into one of life, while their infidelity in the land turned Yhwh's own land of plenty and blessing into an abomination, and consequently a place of death. The force of the accusation in 2:7 is that it is not any land that has been defiled, but *Yhwh's holy land, his* inheritance, which is now an abomination.[28] The responsibility for the desecration is intergenerational. The "you" of v. 7 refers not just to the generation of Jeremiah's time, but to the ancestors who first came into the land.[29] Another way of explaining the people's failure is their loss of memory: "my people have forgotten me, days without number" (2:32). What they have especially forgotten is their history of how Yhwh freed them from Egypt, guided them through the desert, and finally brought them to the land (2:6–7; 13:25; 18:15; 44:9).

The Jeremiah tradition blames the nation's leaders for the disaster, but does not restrict responsibility to them alone. Not only are the priests, rulers, and prophets all condemned in the book (e.g.: 2:8; 8:1; 13:13; 32:32), but the people as a whole do not escape censure (2:26):

> As a thief is shamed when caught, so the house of Israel shall be shamed—they, their kings, their officials, their priests, and their prophets

There are a number of oracles or speeches addressed to the "people of Judah and inhabitants of Jerusalem" (e.g., 4:3; 11:2, 9; 17:25; 18:11; 32:32; 35:13; 36:31). Their abandonment of Yhwh is also the grounds for punishment: "Has a nation changed its gods, even though they are no gods? But my people have changed their glory for something that does not profit"

---

27. As noted by Craigie, Kelley, and Drinkard Jr., *Jeremiah 1–25*, 24–25.

28. The contrast between the ideal of the holiness of Yhwh's land and its reality as an abomination is "as striking and abrasive as can be imagined" (Brueggemann, "Israel's Sense of Place in Jeremiah," 127).

29. Allen, *Jeremiah*, 40.

(2:11). The book also contains denunciations of kings, priests, and prophets, for abandoning the exclusive worship of Yhwh. The Jeremian themes in these early chapters are well summed up as "a corrupt nation and corrupting leadership."[30]

In the book there are individual passages that accuse specific kings, priests, and prophets, of abandoning the exclusive worship of Yhwh. In 15:1–4 total responsibility for the demise of Judah is attributed to Manasseh:

> Then the LORD said to me:
> Though Moses and Samuel stood before me,
> yet my heart would not turn toward this people.
> Send them out of my sight, and let them go!
> I will make them a horror to all the kingdoms of the earth
> because of what King Manasseh son of Hezekiah of Judah did in Jerusalem. (15:1, 4)

Given the connections between the book of Jeremiah and the Deuteronomistic tradition, there is no surprise here, either in the reference to Manasseh, or in the invoking of the memory of Moses and Samuel.[31] Great as they were, even their intercession would now go unheeded.[32] The use of the expression "Send them out of my sight, and let them go!" is reminiscent of Moses' demand to Pharaoh: "let my people go" (Exod 5:1). However, in Jer 15:1 it is "a dismissal from the divine presence."[33] The punishment is a repudiation of the deliverance from Egypt, an "ironic reversal of the exodus myth."[34]

In 21:1—23:8 the kings who ruled from 609 to 597 are denounced by name: Jehoahaz (22:11–22), Jehoiakim (22:18–23), and Jehoiachin (22:24–30). Perhaps the most recalcitrant of these was Jehoiakim, at least according to Jer 36. It narrates how the prophet had dictated his message to his scribe Baruch, who then wrote it down on a scroll, which was then taken and read

---

30. Carroll, *Jeremiah*, 125.

31. There is a widely accepted view by scholars that the book of Jeremiah contains material that is similar, but not identical to that of the Deuteronomists. However, the precise relationship and level of dependence between the Jeremiah tradition and that of the Deuteronomists has been much debated. For a range of views, see e.g., Carroll, *Jeremiah*; McKane, *Jeremiah 1*; E. W. Nicholson, *Preaching to the Exiles*; Thiel, *Jeremia 1–25*.

32. So, Allen, "Ezekiel's Revisionist History," 175; Craigie, Kelley, and Drinkard Jr., *Jeremiah 1–25*, 204.

33. Carroll, *Jeremiah*, 320. For the connection between Jer 15:14 and the Moses-Pharaoh confrontations, see Carroll, *Jeremiah*, 319–20 Hill, *Friend or Foe?* 77.

34. Carroll, *Jeremiah*, 320.

to Jehoiakim. As it was read to him, Jehoiakim cut pieces off the scroll and threw them into the fire (36:23). Even when his court officials urged him not to do it, he refused to listen (v. 25). As a result of the destruction of this first scroll and Jehoiakim's defiance, Jeremiah denounces him: "He shall have no one to sit on the throne of David, and his dead body will be cast out to the heat by day and the frost by night" (v. 30). The Jeremian portrait of the kings here is in stark contrast to the Zion theology. In the latter, the king has the privileged position as Yhwh's anointed servant, whereas Jeremiah reduces the fate of Jehoiakim to that of a donkey: "With the burial of a donkey he shall be buried—dragged off and thrown out beyond the gates of Jerusalem" (22:19).

Another group held responsible for the disaster are the priests. Like the kings, they are often denounced as a group (e.g., 2:24; 6:13; 14:18). Similarly, the prophets as a class are also held responsible (2:26; 6:13; 14:14–18). Chapter 23 contains a long diatribe against Jeremiah's prophetic opponents, whom he likens to the inhabitants of Sodom and Gomorrah (23:14). They were accused of making predictions based on their own delusions, and offering false hope and comfort to their audience (v. 17). One prophetic opponent is named, Hananiah. He contradicted Jeremiah's message of imminent doom and punishment, and predicted that Babylon's control over Judah would last only two years, after which the exiles in Babylon would then return (28:3).

The book of Jeremiah also uses a catechetical devise, the question-and-answer pattern, to give an unambiguous explanation for the disaster and for the fate suffered by its survivors. It is reminiscent of a catechism question followed by a short summary answer. The pattern is found in a number of places in the book.[35] 5:19 is an example:

> And when you say, "Why has the LORD our God done all these things to us?" you shall say to them, "As you have forsaken me and served foreign gods in your land, so you shall serve strangers in a land that is not yours." (5:19)

The pattern usually consists of three elements: a) a question; b) an answer together with an explanation; c) a "restatement of the circumstances

---

35. The pattern occurs in Jer 5:19; 9:11–15; 16:10–13; 22:8–9; 40:2–3, and also in Deut 29:24–25 (MT 29:23–24) and 1 Kgs 9:8. For a description of the pattern, see E. W. Nicholson, *Preaching to the Exiles*, 58–63; Thiel, *Jeremia 1–25*, 295–300. Shorter summaries can be found in Carroll, *Jeremiah*, 242–43; Hill, "Jeremiah 40.1–6," 133–34.

which prompted the question."[36] The question is projected into the future ("And when you say ..."—5:19aβ). The answer can have two temporal aspects. It refers to past behavior ("As you have forsaken me ..."—v. 19bβ), and a future punishment ("so shall you serve strangers in a land not yours"—5:19bγ). In 5:19 an answer is given by a single survivor ("you"—singular), to a question posed by a group of survivors ("you"—plural).[37] The answer makes it clear that the people as a whole ("you"—plural) are guilty of abandoning Yhwh and worshipping other deities.[38]

The Book of Ezekiel: A People Corrupt from Birth

The book of Ezekiel gives us a revisionist view of Israel's history, and so is radically different. It lays the blame for the Babylonian invasion and conquest at the feet of the whole nation, a people who were corrupt not only in the years leading up to the invasion, but from their very beginning. Where the book of Jeremiah portrayed Israel's history as consisting of two parts, the period of fidelity to Yhwh in the wilderness and that of infidelity when they came into the land, Ezekiel describes the people as sinful from their birth. The book also has its own particular view about the exile. The beginning of the exilic period is usually said to be 587, because after that there was no functioning temple, no Davidic monarchy, and no Judah as a nation in its own right. However, Ezekiel was among those deported to Babylon in 597, so the book's chronological superscriptions use 597 as their reference point. The book has a clearly organized structure, consisting predominantly oracles of judgment against Judah in chapters 1–24, oracles against the nations in chapters 25–32, oracles of deliverance in chapters 33–39, and a vision of a new temple in chapters 40–48.

---

36. E. W. Nicholson, *Preaching to the Exiles*, 59.

37. Unlike English, Hebrew has different forms for the second person singular and plural instances of verbs.

38. There are variations of the pattern in other places. Where the question in 5:19 is framed in general terms, in Jer 9:12 (9:11 MT) it is about the fate of the land: "Why is the land ruined and laid waste like a wilderness." Sometimes the identity of the speakers varies. In 9:12 the question is posed by an anonymous individual, in 16:10 by the people ("you"—plural), while in 22:8 it comes from "many nations" who are portrayed as passing by the ruined city of Jerusalem. The identity of those who answer also varies. In 9:13 (MT 9:12) it is Yhwh who answers, whereas in 16:11 it is Jeremiah, in 22:8 the "many nations," and in 40:2–3 it is the Babylonian commander Nebuzaradan.

The book consists largely of long oracles. Their length and complexity have led to the suggestion that their original form was written, rather than spoken.[39] Their length and complexity have also given rise to much discussion about the book's compositional history and its levels of redaction.[40] In what follows my approach is to recognize that there are various redactional levels, and that they are generally in harmony with texts that reflect the earliest levels of the tradition.[41]

The key texts for consideration here are Ezek 16, 20, and 23.[42] They provide graphic and disturbing descriptions of the people's total corruption, and their sorry history of infidelity to Yhwh. However, it is first necessary for us to look at the book's perspective on the exiles in Babylon and the people who remained behind in Judah after 597.

The Communities in Babylon and Judah.

The book makes a clear distinction between those exiled to Babylon after 592 and those who remained in Judah. While both groups are guilty of infidelity to Yhwh, the book clearly identifies those in Babylon as favored by Yhwh, and those in Judah as continuing in their evil ways.

Ezekiel 1:1 locates the prophet in Babylon "among the exiles."[43] The Hebrew word commonly translated as "exiles" in the book is used only of the community in Babylon. Where the book refers to others who departed willingly or unwillingly from Judah, it refers to them as being scattered or dispersed. Their situation is referred to as diaspora. Only the Babylonian group are called "exiles."[44] 1:2, the superscription for a series of oracles,

---

39. So, Ellen F. Davis, *Swallowing the Scroll, Prophecy*, 37–39.

40. A summary of the common approaches is given by Apóstolo, "Imagining Ezekiel"; Ehrlich, "Ezekiel," 120–22.

41. Following the approach of Joyce that the book may have had a long redactional history, but "because of the marked homogeneity of the Ezekiel tradition, in which secondary material bears an unusually close 'family resemblance' to primary" (Joyce, *Ezekiel*, 12).

42. A brief summary of the portrayal of Israel's past in Ezekiel 16, 20 and 23 is given by Luc, "A Theology of Ezekiel: God's Name and Israel's History," 138–39.

43. Hebrew: בתוך־הגולה.

44. The Hebrew word in question is גולה, a singular noun, derived from the verb גלה. In its *hifil* form it means "to lead into exile," and occurs with this meaning only once in the book (39:28). Its *qal* form, which means "to uncover," is found especially in chapters 16 and 23, usually with the nuance of being naked.

refers to the fifth year of the "exile of king Jehoiachin." Ezekiel was one of the exiles who came with Jehoiachin in 592. Their situation is referred to "our exile" (33:21; 40:1), and he is "part and parcel of that community."[45] He is sent to "the house of Israel," an expression that can refer to Ezekiel's fellow exiles (e.g., 2:3; 3:1), or those who were left behind in Judah after 597 (4:3, 4). Both were guilty of infidelity to Yhwh, but as our next chapter shows, the exiles in Babylon were offered a future whereas those left behind were offered none.

The differences between the two communities is more than geographical.[46] Rather, they are profoundly theological. Behind them is the question about identity: who is the true Israel. The conflict surfaces in 11:15:

> O mortal one, to your brothers, even your brothers, the men of your kinsfolk, and to the whole house of Israel, the inhabitants of Jerusalem have said: They have gone far away from the LORD; to us this land has been given to us to possess. (11:15)

So, the inhabitants of Jerusalem—i.e., those who remained in the land after 597—believe that the exiles in Babylon are the guilty party. Living outside the land means they have been abandoned by Yhwh. Those who remain therefore want nothing to do with the exiles: "they have gone far away from the LORD" (v. 15). However, the group that are disowned by Yhwh are not the exiles, but those who remained in Judah. *They*, according to Ezekiel, are the ones guilty of "detestable things" and "abominations," and will suffer punishment from Yhwh (v. 21). In 33:24 a claim similar to that in 11:15 is put on the lips of those who remained behind:

> Mortal, the inhabitants of these waste places in the land of Israel keep saying, "Abraham was only one man, yet he got possession of the land; but we are many; the land is surely given us to possess." (33:24)

Those left behind claim a connection to Abraham. As his descendants the land should be theirs. Yhwh's response, however, is to accuse them of sexual offences and other actions that defile the land. They are further threatened, not with exile, but with the total destruction of the land, which will be made devoid of any inhabitants. It will be left as "a desolation and a waste" (33:28).

---

45. Rom-Shiloni, "Ezekiel," 8.
46. On what follows, see Rom-Shiloni, "Ezekiel," 11–20.

Yhwh's favor is with the exiles in Babylon. Even though they are separated from the Jerusalem temple, they are not cut off from Yhwh. Ezekiel's portrayal of two different groups reflects the intra-community conflicts that began after 597 and continued long after the demise of the Babylonians.

Ezekiel 16, 23

Ezekiel 16 is the longest chapter in the book. It is in the form of a prophetic lawsuit.[47] The idea is that Yhwh takes his people to court and puts them on trial.[48] In Ezek 16 the accused is Jerusalem, who is portrayed as woman, and represents the whole people.[49] In vv. 3b–34 we find Yhwh's accusation about their behavior. Their sin is their rejection of Yhwh and their worship of other deities.[50] As part of the accusation, Ezekiel rewrites the people's history to show that they are sinful and corrupt from the beginning. He starts with their origins:

> Thus says the Lord God to Jerusalem:
> Your origin and your birth were in the land of the Canaanites;
> your father was an Amorite, and your mother a Hittite.[51] (16:3)

As a newborn, Jerusalem is abandoned by her mother (vv. 4–6), but her life is saved by Yhwh, who in his compassion takes her in and cares for her.[52] Although Yhwh's action means he adopts the infant, she continues to be an outsider, and never really belongs to the family.[53] Yet she is dressed in rich beauty, and her clothing "is more elegant than any other described in

---

47. Block, *The Book of Ezekiel: Chapters 1–24*, 497. For the chapter's structure and divisions see Maier, *Daughter Zion, Mother Zion*, 112–13.

48. For greater detail of the structure of the prophetic lawsuit, see Block, *The Book of Ezekiel: Chapters 1–24*, 460–62; also Allen, *Ezekiel 1–19*, 232–33.

49. Joyce, *Ezekiel*, 130. For further on the imagery of Jerusalem as a woman, see Galambush, *Jerusalem*, 20–23, 89–90.

50. The meaning of "lovers" in vv. 37–39 may be either foreign deities or foreign enemies (Allen, *Ezekiel 1–19*, 235; Galambush, *Jerusalem*, 97–98).

51. The reference to Jerusalem's Canaanite origins is historically accurate, as pointed out by Odell, *Ezekiel*, 188. She also notes how the terms "Hittites," "Amorites," and "Canaanites" are often used to describe Israel's enemies (Odell, *Ezekiel*, 188–89).

52. On the renunciation of Jerusalem by her parents, Galambush, *Jerusalem*, 91–92.

53. She remains the outsider because of "her foreign descent, her abandonment after birth, and her polluted status lying in her birth blood" (Maier, *Daughter Zion, Mother Zion*, 114).

the Bible."⁵⁴ Yhwh enters into a marriage covenant with her (vv. 8–14), but Jerusalem's response is to behave like a prostitute (vv. 15–34).

The image of the people of Israel as a prostitute or unfaithful wife is not peculiar to the book of Ezekiel, but is found in both Hosea and Jeremiah.⁵⁵ The function of the imagery is to highlight the people's infidelity to Yhwh, and their turning to other deities. Yhwh the husband complains that all the beautiful gifts he had given to his beloved have been handed on by her to her new lovers (vv. 17–18). The gifts referred to here are mostly jewelry and clothing. Oil and incense, which are a reference to worship, are also mentioned (v. 18). Originally intended for use in the worship of Yhwh, they are now available for people in their veneration of other deities.⁵⁶ Furthermore, in the context of worship, Ezek 20 also accuses the people of killing and sacrificing their firstborn children, who are not just their offspring but who, as firstborn, belong to Yhwh: "You slaughtered *my* children" (v. 21; emphasis mine).⁵⁷

The distinctive nature of Ezekiel's portrayal of Israel's origins is highlighted when compared to other similar OT traditions. According to Gen 11–17, the people of Israel are the descendants of Abraham, while theological traditions associated with the exodus place their origins in the deliverance from Egypt. Ezekiel's understanding is radically different. While it may be historically true that Jerusalem was originally a Canaanite city, Ezekiel's interests are not historical. His aim is to undermine any understanding of Israel as a people who were specially chosen and loved by Yhwh. Instead he wants to demonstrate that their corruption goes right back to their very beginnings: "Like mother, like daughter" (v. 44).⁵⁸ The trashing of Jerusalem's origins is continued by Ezekiel's portrait of her sisters. The older one is Samaria (v. 46). Denunciations of the Northern Kingdom are not uncommon, and Samaria's fate was used by the prophets to warn Judah to amend her ways (e.g., 2 Kgs 17). Now in Ezek 16:51–52 Jerusalem's

---

54. Galambush, *Jerusalem*, 95; Odell, *Ezekiel*, 190.

55. Ezekiel adopts but then modifies the harlotry imagery found in Hosea and Jeremiah (Galambush, *Jerusalem*, 78–88; Odell, *Ezekiel*, 182).

56. Joyce, *Ezekiel*, 132.

57. For further, see Block, *The Book of Ezekiel: Chapters 1-24*, 489–91; Joyce, *Ezekiel*, 132.

58. In the context of chapter 16, "'Canaanites', 'Hittites' and 'Amorites' represent human depravity at its worst" Block, *The Book of Ezekiel: Chapters 1-24*, 475. As Block also notes, Deut 7:2 mandates the extermination of these three ethnic groups (Block, *The Book of Ezekiel: Chapters 1-24*, 475).

behavior is compared to that of Samaria. Whatever the failings of the latter, Jerusalem has "committed more abominations than they [Samaria], and have made your sisters appear righteous by all the abominations that you have committed" (v. 51). The unflattering comparison is now followed by something far more outrageous. Jerusalem's younger sister is now introduced. Her name is Sodom! Guilty as she is, "your sister Sodom and her daughters have not done as you and your daughters have done" (v. 48).

Ezekiel's portrait of the people as shameless and totally corrupt is made more unpalatable by the explicitly sexual imagery found in the chapter. The books of both Hosea and Jeremiah portray the people's relationship with Yhwh as a marriage, and use sexual imagery, but nowhere near the frequency found in Ezekiel. Its aim is to produce a feeling of disgust at the people's infidelity to Yhwh, to humiliate and shame them in the hope that they will repent.[59]

Similar imagery is used to describe the people's failures in chapter 23. Like chapter 16 it uses the same literary form, a prophetic lawsuit, but with an extended indictment (16:6-34; 23:5-21) and announcement of punishment (16:22-43; 23:22-25).[60] It claims that both Israel's origins and history of infidelity began in Egypt, a point of view found also in chapter 20.[61] After an introductory verse, Ezek 23 introduces two sisters named Oholah and Oholibah, who represent Samaria and Jerusalem respectively (v. 4).[62] They begin their promiscuous behavior in Egypt. Oholibah is more promiscuous than her older sister, whose behavior leads to her demise at the hands of the Assyrians in 721 BCE. Besides consorting with the Egyptians and the Assyrians, Oholibah brings the Babylonians to her bed (v. 17). The imagery of sexual promiscuity here is a metaphor for the defiling the temple by their syncretistic worship, the practice of child sacrifice, and the failure to observe the sabbath (vv. 37-39).

---

59. For some important reflections on the sexual imagery in Ezekiel, which is so confronting and offensive to contemporary readers, see Maier, *Daughter Zion, Mother Zion*, 134-40, 216-17.

60. Block, *The Book of Ezekiel: Chapters 1-24*, 729.

61. The similarities and differences between chapters 16 and 23 are outlined by Block, *The Book of Ezekiel: Chapters 1-24*, 729.

62. Oholah means "her tent"; Oholibah "my tent is in her." Suggestions about the significance of these names are discussed by Allen, *Ezekiel 20-48*, 48; Block, *The Book of Ezekiel: Chapters 1-24*, 735-36; Galambush, *Jerusalem*, 111 n.58.

Ezekiel 20

Like chapter 16, Ezek 20 presents a revisionist view of Israel's history, but without the personification of Jerusalem and the accompanying sexual imagery.[63] While the oracle in chapter 16 is directed towards the community in Jerusalem, that in chapter 20 is addressed to the community in Babylon (20:1). Here they are addressed as "house of Israel" (20:30, 31, 44) or "house of Jacob" (v. 5). The text is long, but can be divided into a preamble (vv. 1–4), and a long Yhwh speech (vv. 5–44), which in turn can be further divided into vv. 5–31 and 32–44.[64] In chapter 20 also, Israel's history begins with the time in Egypt:

> On that day I swore to them that I would bring them out of the land of Egypt into a land that I had searched out for them, a land flowing with milk and honey, the most glorious of all lands.
> And I said to them, Cast away the detestable things your eyes feast on, every one of you, and do not defile yourselves with the idols of Egypt; I am the LORD your God. (20:6–7)

In the books of Genesis and Exodus there is no indication that the Israelites worshipped the Egyptian deities, or were in anyway unfaithful to Yhwh while in that country. In contrast, Ezek 20 accuses them of chasing after foreign deities even before they left Egypt.

The chapter identifies different generations in Israel's history, and portrays every one of them as corrupt and defiled. The first generation are those in Egypt (vv. 5–9). The next generation are those in the wilderness (vv. 10–17), followed by their children (vv. 18–26). Then comes the two generations who lived in the land, "your ancestors" (v. 27), and then Ezekiel's own generation (vv. 27–31).[65] Each is accused of rejecting Yhwh's laws (vv. 8, 13, 21, 28, 31). Apart from Ezekiel's generation, the previous ones were all threatened by Yhwh with a judgment that was never realized. What is interesting here is the motive behind Yhwh's change of heart towards Ezekiel's generation:

---

63. Block, *The Book of Ezekiel: Chapters 1–24*, 149.

64. For these divisions and more on the structure of the chapter, see Block, *The Book of Ezekiel: Chapters 1–24*, 611–12. For a detailed treatment of the divisions and structure of the chapter, see Allen, "Ezekiel's Revisionist History"; Krüger, "Transformation," 160.

65. Rom-Shiloni, "Facing Destruction and Exile," 200; Strine, "The Role of Repentance," 483–84. The structuring of the generations is based on Num 14 (Block, *The Book of Ezekiel: Chapters 1–24*, 633; Strine, "The Role of Repentance," 486).

> I acted for the sake of my name, that it should not be profaned in the sight of the nations among whom they lived. (v. 9)

A similar pattern can be seen in vv. 14 and 22. There is no suggestion of repentance by any of the generations, nor any compassion by Yhwh. Rather the change of heart came from a desire to preserve his prestige and reputation among the nations.[66]

In response to the behavior of the children of the wilderness generation, Yhwh gives them what v. 25 calls "statutes that were not good, and ordinances by which they could not live." It is as if Israel's complete corruption from its beginnings meant that giving them laws that were good and life-giving was pointless and a waste of time.[67] Although its interpretation has been much disputed, v. 25 is consistent with a picture of a totally corrupt Israel, and the suggestion that their god had given up on them.[68] Compared to the explanations offered for the disaster of 587 by the Deuteronomistic History and the book of Jeremiah, that proposed by Ezekiel is the most radical and disturbing.

SUMMARY

The disaster of 587 undermined the foundations of Judah's identity and left it with critical questions about its future. It triggered an outpouring of grief and confusion, which we find in the book of Lamentations. The book raises but does not answer a question that was too painful to consider: has Yhwh completely abandoned us? So the book does not end even with a question but with words that are indefinite and unfinished: "unless you have utterly rejected us, and are angry with us beyond measure . . ." (Lam 5:22).

Besides expressing their grief, the survivors also looked for explanations about the cause of such a catastrophe. We find them in the Deuteronomistic History, and in the books of Jeremiah and Ezekiel. All of the three

---

66. "If God destroys the Israelites in Egypt he will be seen by the nations as not being able to keep to his word, to carry out what he intended to do. The destruction of Israelites would not be seen as a justified punishment, but as the weakness and powerlessness of Yahweh" (Wong, "Profanation/Sanctification," 217–18). See also Rom-Shiloni, "Facing Destruction and Exile," 200.

67. "Thus, even the law itself was infected by their apostasy" (Albertz, *Israel in Exile*, 365).

68. The differing interpretations of v. 25 can be found in Hahn and Bergsma, "What Laws Were 'Not Good'?"

contain a retrospective view of Judah's history. The Deuteronomists put the responsibility for the disaster on the kings (both of Judah and the former northern kingdom of Israel). It was their infidelity to Yhwh and their worship of alien deities that caused the catastrophe of 587. In a later nomistic edition of the history, the Deuteronomists extended their understanding of the cause to include the whole community. It was not just the kings who abandoned the exclusive worship of Yhwh, but so did the community at large. It was not just a matter of corrupt rulers, but also a corrupt people.

The book of Jeremiah also laid the blame at the feet of the whole nation. It contrasted the fidelity of the generations that Yhwh led through the desert to the infidelity of the generations who occupied the promised land. The book highlights the irony that in the wilderness—a place of death—the people found life. In the promised land—intended as a place of life and blessing—the nation is now destined for death.

The book of Ezekiel presents the most radical portrait of Judah as it allocates responsibility for the disaster. The history of the people is one of corruption from its very beginnings, right back to its time in Egypt before the exodus. The book also uses sexual imagery to portray the people's inherently and unfaithful character. The people are also represented by the feminine figure of Jerusalem. She is portrayed as an unwanted Canaanite baby whom Yhwh adopts. In this sense she is an outsider and never really one of the family. As an adult she is a promiscuous, unfaithful wife. As in Jeremiah, the failure of the people is their worship of deities other than Yhwh.

The result of the Babylonian conquest was the destruction of much of Judah's infrastructure and the deportation of a segment of its population. Although the number of the deportees was relatively small as a percentage of the total population, as exiles in Babylon they played a very significant role in the emergence of a future community. So, our next chapter is about them and their life in Babylon.

Chapter 4

THE COMMUNITY IN BABYLON AND THE EMERGENCE OF HOPE

IN THIS CHAPTER OUR focus now shifts to the community in Babylon. We will explore the situation of the deportees from Judah, the crisis they faced, and how they responded. How did they live in this new situation of forced displacement? How did they understand or imagine their future? Did they envisage living the rest of their lives in Babylon, or was there any hope of a return to the homeland?

In the first part of this chapter we make use of recent archaeological evidence that has given us a better picture of the deportees' situation in Babylon. In the second part we look at three responses to the crises: a) assimilation, reflected in Jeremiah's letter to the exiles (Jer 29:4–7); b) separation, expressed in the observance of sabbath, dietary laws, and circumcision, as understood in the Priestly tradition; c) confrontation, as found in Deutero-Isaiah's diatribes against idol worship and the Babylonian deities. The third part of the chapter is an account of the different visions of the future that emerged in the community. Here we look at the promise of the land to Abraham and his descendants in Gen 17, the wonderfully poetic portrait of a return to the homeland in Deutero-Isaiah, and the visions of the future found in the book of Ezekiel.

THE COMMUNITY IN BABYLON AND THE EMERGENCE OF HOPE

THE CRISIS OF EXILE

Modern studies point out some of the issues that forcibly displaced peoples have to face. Especially apt, when considering the displacement of the exiles from Judah, is the diminishment of resources and security.[1] Security in the past had come from the Zion theology. The gift of the land gave them the security of housing and food, together with a network of social relationships in the villages, towns, or cities where they lived. The defeat of Judah's armies left them bereft of security and at the mercy of the conquerors. Although we know nothing about the conditions under which they came from Judah to Babylon, history would suggest that such forced marches were brutal affairs, marked by starvation, violence, and the deaths of significant numbers.

The other significant crisis they faced was their belief in Yhwh. The Babylonian conquest raised questions about their religion. Were the Babylonian deities simply more powerful than Yhwh? Or was Yhwh punishing Judah, and why? Or, even worse, was Lam 5:22 right when it intimated that Yhwh might have completely abandoned them?[2] We will now sketch some features of life in Babylon, and the resolution of the critical issues it faced.

Life in Babylon

The exiles from Judah came in three waves: in 597, 587, and 582. Those who came in 597 were from the elite, and they were the first to confront a situation that was unknown and traumatic. Drawn from the upper classes in Judah, they now found themselves, as forced laborers, to be down near the bottom of the pile.[3] Their experience of life in Babylon would have at least provided some support for the next wave. The 587 group were perhaps the most traumatized because they had witnesses or experienced the destruction of Jerusalem and all the horrors that accompanied the siege of the city.[4] The 582 group may have consisted of trouble-makers, involved

---

1. Ames, "The Cascading Effects of Exile," 175–77.
2. On Lam 5:22, see pages 24–25 above.
3. Ahn, *Exile as Forced Migrations*, 49.
4. They experienced "not only the destruction of Jerusalem, but moreover, the atrocious decapitation, mutilation, or even burning of little children—the loss of an entire generation" (Ahn, *Exile as Forced Migrations*, 74).

in some way with the murder of Gedaliah, or who were brought to Babylon to top up the supply of forced labor.[5]

Historical evidence about the exiles in Babylon is rather limited, but some recent discoveries give us some insight into life in the latter years of the neo-Babylonian era. The Babylonians settled ethnic minorities in their own cohesive groups, and allowed them their own organization.[6] Probably, for except Jehoiachin and some members of his household, the majority of the deportees were settled in a place called Tel-abib, along the River Chebar, near the city of Nippur.[7] In past research descriptions of the trauma experienced by the exiles have been predominantly based on indirect evidence—i.e., interpretations of exilic texts read through the lens of contemporary trauma studies.[8] Now we have more direct evidence about the exiles' life in Babylon which come from texts originating in the latter years of the Babylonian era. The main sources for information about Judahites in Babylon during the Neo-Babylonian period came from either the Weidner Tablets or the Murašû archive. The tablets give information about King Jehoiachin, which can be dated to around 592 BCE, while the archive's earliest references are to the mid-fifth century BCE.[9]

More recently a series of tablets have been discovered and are in the process of being published. Dating back to 498, the Yahudu tablets point to the existence of various Judahite settlements around Babylon, including one called *āl-Yā hūdu*, a place previously unknown. Its name means "the city of Judah."[10] The tablets provide evidence of Judahites living in Babylon, intermarrying, and engaging in business. The settlements were agricultural, places where they could cultivate land and grow food for themselves. In summarizing the evidence of the Yahudu tablets, Jonathan Stökl identifies three different Judahite groups in Babylon; "1) upper class Judahites at the

---

5. Ahn, *Exile as Forced Migrations*, 65.

6. Albertz, *Israel in Exile*, 100; Betylon, "Neo-Babylonians Military Operations," 265; Vanderhooft, "Babylonian Strategies," 255.

7. Hayes and Miller, *Israelite and Judean History*, 482; Betylon, "Neo-Babylonians Military Operations," 265.

8. Such as Boda et al., *The Prophets Speak on Forced Migration*; Smith-Christopher, *Exile*.

9. For a brief summary, see Nissinen, "Ezekiel," 88–90; Delorme, "Identity Construction," 128–30. For a more extensive treatments of the Yahudu tablets, see e.g., Abraham, "West Semitic and Judean Brides"; Beaulieu, "Yahwistic Names"; Pearce, "New Evidence"; Pearce, "Identifying," 8–11.

10. Pearce, "New Evidence," 400.

royal court in Babylon, 2) traders throughout the Babylonian cities, and 3) subsistence farmers in the Nippur region."[11] References in the book of Ezekiel also suggest that there was also a worshipping community, headed by a group of elders.[12]

A Crisis of Faith

The deportees' initial experience in Babylon would have been one of disillusionment and confusion. Babylon was one of the great cities of the ancient world. In comparison, Jerusalem was no more than a rustic village. Life in Babylon presented two crises for them: the validity of their Yahwistic faith, and the question of their future. The conquest of Jerusalem and the destruction of its temples raised serious questions for them about their belief in Yhwh.[13] The conquest showed that the Babylonian deities were, after all, more powerful than Yhwh. The destruction of the Jerusalem temple indicated either that he had either been defeated, or had abandoned the place and, by implication, the people who were his adherents.

Evidence for the crisis of faith is found in Isa 40–55. Typical of the doubts expressed were "my way is hidden from the LORD, and my right is disregarded by my God" (Isa 40:27). Another complaint was that "the LORD has forsaken me, my LORD has forgotten me" (49:14). The seeming impotence of Yhwh is also raised, that his hand "is shortened, that it cannot redeem" (50:2). Besides Isa 40–55, the Priestly parts of the Pentateuch were also developed as responses to the crisis of faith, and the figure of Abraham became important in the community's vision of the future.

RESPONSES TO THE CRISIS

Responses to the crisis varied. Some related to the situation at hand in Babylon, while others were about the future. In this section we look at three responses that dealt with the situation at hand: assimilation, separation,

---

11. Stökl, "Ezekiel's Access to Babylonian Culture," 227.

12. As reflected in Ezek 8:1; 14:1; 20:1. See also Albertz, *Israel in Exile*, 100–104. For an extensive discussion of the structural adaptations made by the exiles in Babylon, see Smith, *The Religion of the Landless*, 93–108 For a further summary of the exiles' life in Babylon, see Gerstenberger, *Israel in the Persian Period*, 122–26.

13. Blenkinsopp, *Isaiah 40–55*, 104–5.

and confrontation. Then later we will examine the visions of the future that emerged from the community of the exiles.

Assimilation

Perhaps the earliest text that contains a response is the letter of Jeremiah (chapter 29). The letter was written against the background of the political unrest that occurred around 595–594 in Syria-Palestine, shortly after the 597 deportees arrived in Babylon. The unrest was the result of the decision of Judah's king, Zedekiah, and rulers of neighboring countries subjugated by Babylon to rebel by refusing to pay taxes. It fuelled the hope that their stay in Babylon would be short, as predicted by Jeremiah's prophetic opponents, such as Hananiah who predicted that the deportees stay in Babylon would last only two years (Jer 28:3).[14] The advice Jeremiah gave to the deportees around 592 was just the opposite. He proposed a radical form of integration:

> Build houses and live in them;
> plant gardens and eat what they produce.
> Take wives and have sons and daughters;
> take wives for your sons, and give your daughters in marriage,
> that they may bear sons and daughters;
> multiply there, and do not decrease.
> But seek the welfare of the city
> where I have sent you into exile,
> and pray to the LORD on its behalf,
> for in its welfare you will find your welfare. (29:5–7)

As I have written elsewhere, the language of this advice is not simply pragmatic, given in the face of political and military impotence, but is utterly radical and almost blasphemous.[15] Rather than pray for the welfare or peace of Jerusalem (v. 7), the deportees must now accept that the city of their welfare or peace is to be Babylon. Furthermore, it is in this unclean and alien place, and not in the Jerusalem temple that they will find Yhwh.[16] The building of houses and inhabiting them, the planting of gardens and enjoying their produce, the taking of wives and husbands and bearing

---

14. For the historical background of Jer 28, see e.g., Holladay, *Jeremiah 2*, 140; Keown, Scalise, and Smothers, *Jeremiah 26–52*, 69; Thompson, *Jeremiah*, 544–45.
15. Hill, *Friend or Foe?* 146–54.
16. Hill, *Friend or Foe?* 151.

children—these are all blessings that came with living in the land of Judah (Deut 20:5–8; Isa 65:21–23). The command to carry out these activities *in Babylon* is saying that Babylon should now supplant Judah as the exiles' home.[17] Jeremiah 29:5–7 was an expression of the assimilation option, and the Yahudu tablets indicate that at least some of the exiles took that course of action.

Separation

Among the exiles were members of the Jerusalem priesthood, who brought with them traditions associated with the rituals, worship, and narratives about pre-587 Judah and its origins. They were focussed on creating an identity, based on separation, and tailored to the life as exiles in Babylon. At the same time they also held the hope of a return to the homeland. The Priestly theologians (P) retrieved practices and beliefs from the past and reinterpreted them to provide elements of identity adapted to a community's new situation.[18] The traditions they reinterpreted were the sabbath, dietary laws, and circumcision. These became markers of identity for a community living in Babylon, which saw itself as distinctive, markedly different from the surrounding society and culture.

Genesis 1:1—2:4a, with its understanding of creation and the significance of the sabbath is a P text developed in Babylon. It provided the theological underpinning for P's construction of a new identity for the exiles. Genesis 1:2 refers to a God who can bring order out of chaos. This was an important idea because in Jer 4:22–27 the impending destruction of Judah by the Babylonians is described as a reversal of Gen 1:2: "I looked on the earth, and it was waste and void."[19] Yhwh, who acted to destroy Judah, could also create and bring new life. The account of creation comes to its climax with the observance of the sabbath by Yhwh (2:2–3). What is commonly overlooked in these verses is the relationship between the first six days and the seventh. The text does not tell us that Yhwh worked for six days, and then rested from his work on the sabbath, as if the days for work

---

17. For further on Jeremiah's letter, see Ahn, *Exile as Forced Migrations*, 138–41; Ames, "The Cascading Effects of Exile," 182–85.

18. Boorer, *Vision*, 101.

19. Unlike the English translations, the Hebrew of both Gen 1:2 and Jer 4:23 both refer to the earth as תהו ובהו ("formlessness and emptiness").

were completely separate from the day of rest. According to 2:2, Yhwh's rest *completed* the work of creation.[20]

In Gen 1:1—2:4 P took an old tradition and reinterpreted it for a new situation.[21] In earlier legislation the observance of the sabbath was intended to provide physical rest for the community, its slaves, and even its animals (Exod 20:10). Besides the idea of physical rest, Deut 5:12-15 sees sabbath observance as a way of remembering the time of slavery in Egypt and the deliverance by Yhwh. For P the reason for observance is different. Since the God they believed in rested on the sabbath, so should they. Also, since sabbath was not something practiced by the Babylonians, it became a distinctive identity marker of the exiles as a minority group living at the center of the foreign empire.

Besides the theme of creation on Gen 1:1—2:4a, there is another important idea that is relevant for our understanding of the community in Babylon. This is the theme of *separation*, which occurs in vv. 4, 6, and 7. Yhwh's first act of separation establishes the basic rhythm of day and night: "God separated the light from the darkness" (v. 4).[22] Verses 6-7 are about the separation of the waters, and the creation of the sky. Next the waters under the sky and the dry land appears (v. 8). Now the waters have their assigned place. The idea of separation is central to these verses of the narrative:

> Separation is part of the first three works of creation. P is saying by this that the world only became the world by separation and only remains the world as long as separation lasts.[23]

Furthermore, the idea of separation is implied in P's account of the sabbath. It means that there two kinds of days. There are the days of work, and then there is the day, different from the others, in which work is completed by rest.

Among the community of the exiles circumcision also became an identity marker. The practice had existed in Israel for many years, and was practiced not only by them but also by their neighbors, as Jer 9:26 shows.[24] An exception was the Philistines who were routinely denounced

---

20. For further on this, see Westermann, *Genesis 1-11*, 89-91.

21. On the idea that sabbath is not an exilic invention, see Brettler, "Judaism," 436-37.

22. "The separation of light and darkness sets in motion this rhythmic polarity which will always belong to creation" (Westermann, *Genesis 1-11*, 114).

23. Westermann, *Genesis 1-11*, 117.

24. See the extended discussion in Faust, "The Bible, Archaeology, and the Practice

as "uncircumcised." However, circumcision was not practiced in Babylon, so in that context it became a distinctive identity marker for the exiles.[25]

Like circumcision, observance of the sabbath by the Judahite community in Babylon was an identity marker, which showed them to be separate and different from those who surrounded them.[26] The idea of separation is also central to Lev 11, which contains dietary regulations. Here the role of the priests is to make a distinction "between the unclean and the clean" (11:46; also 10:10).

Confrontation

Another strategy used to address the anxieties of the exiles was confrontation. It took the form of parodies that satirized and ridiculed both the Babylonian deities and their worshipers, and confronted head-on the temptations of the exiles to abandon Yhwh and worship the Babylonian deities. Isaiah 44:9–20 and 47:1–6 are good example of the strategy.[27]

44:9–20 are preceded by a call on the community to abandon their fears and to trust in Yhwh's power as the sovereign God and creator (vv. 1–8). The polemic in vv. 9–20 does not focus on idolatry as such, but rather on the makers of idols. It lampoons the belief that someone can take a piece of wood, cut it in half, use one half on which to cook a meal, and turn the other half into a god and worship it. Idol-making is foolish and an act of delusion:

> No one considers, nor is there knowledge or discernment to say,
> "Half of it I burned in the fire; I also baked bread on its coals,
> I roasted meat and have eaten.
> Now shall I make the rest of it an abomination?
> Shall I fall down before a block of wood?" (v. 19)

The doubts of the exiles are challenged as the prophet points out the blind stupidity of anyone who worships idols: "A deluded mind has led him

---

of Circumcision."

25. Albertz, *History 2*, 407–8.
26. Albertz, *Israel in Exile*, 107.
27. "The continual and detailed controversy with idolatry would seem to reflect an eyewitness account of Babylonian practices, which viewed the making of idols partly as a ridiculous folly, but partly still as a threat" (Childs, *Isaiah*, 310). Similarly, see also Albertz, *Israel in Exile*, 396.

astray, and he cannot save himself or say 'Is not this thing in my right hand a fraud?'" (v. 20).

Unlike 44:9–20, the polemic in 46:1–7 is specifically about the Babylonian deities Bel and Nebo. Bel is a title of Marduk, the supreme deity in the Babylonian pantheon, and Nebo is his son.[28] Verses 1–2 imagine that Babylon has been defeated and Nebo and Bel are being carried away to some safe place. Their helplessness is then contrasted with Yhwh's active power. Bel and Nebo are passive figures, incapable of moving and who needed to be carried. In contrast, Yhwh is not helpless and passive. As vv. 3–4 show, instead of being carried, he is the one who does the carrying. From birth to old age Israel has been created and carried by him (v. 4): "I have made, and I will bear; I will carry and will save."[29] Verses 6–7 resume a theme from 44:9–20, the stupidity of those who make and worship idols. According to these verses, it was not just wood, but also gold and silver were used by craftsmen to fashion idols. Despite the further expense involved by using silver or gold, the idol was still useless. It could not move, did not answer when called on, and was incapable of saving anyone (v. 7). Verses 8–13 then reaffirm Yhwh's incomparable power: "I am God, and there is no other" (v. 9). Chapter 46 then concludes on an expectant note about the exiles' destiny: "I bring near my deliverance, it is not far off, and my salvation will not tarry" (v. 13).

THE VISION OF THE FUTURE—THE END OF EXILE?

At some point in time a belief about a return to the homeland emerged in the community. We do not know whether political events alone gave rise to the prophecies about Cyrus in Isa 40–55, or whether the prophet had some insight into the future.[30] Regardless of how the belief emerged, in Isa 40–55 it is clearly linked to the appearance of the Persian emperor Cyrus,

---

28. Blenkinsopp, *Isaiah 40–55*, 106–7, 267.

29. So, Blenkinsopp, *Isaiah 40–55*, 268–69.

30. The prophecies about Cyrus touch on the thorny question of the relationship between prophecy and fulfillment. In the present context, Ackroyd's remarks are worth noting: "The interlinkage between prophecy and event is really more subtle that a simple time sequence" (Ackroyd, *Exile and Restoration*, 132). As he also notes about prophecy in general, and about the Cyrus predictions in particular, "the events foretold are not left up in the air, but attached to the realities of the political situation, though not limited by them" (Ackroyd, *Exile and Restoration*, 131). Similarly, see Childs, *Isaiah*, 362.

who defeated and occupied Babylon in 539.³¹ In this section we examine the vision of the future under two headings. One is the promise of land and descendants to Abraham in the book of Genesis. The other is the prophecies of deliverance found in Isa 40–55.

Abraham and the Promises of Land

The P tradition's understanding of the promise of the land to Abraham is found in Gen 17.³² The chapter consists of an introduction (vv. 1–3a), followed by a speech of Yhwh, which divides into three: promise (vv. 3b–8), command (vv. 9–14), and promise (vv. 15–21).³³

Verses 3b–8 contains Yhwh's promise that Abraham's descendants will be "a multitude of nations" (v. 5), which repeats the same promise already found in v. 4. The promise that he will possess the land of Canaan comes only in v. 8, at the end of the section. The reference to the gift of land is framed by assurances of Yhwh's presence with Abraham and his descendants: "I will be God to you" (v. 7), and "I will be their God" (v. 8). The promise of land is "enclosed within the promise of divine presence."³⁴ It contrasts Abraham's present situation, "the land of your sojourning," with his future when the land of Canaan will be his as "an everlasting possession." The Hebrew word translated here as "sojourning" comes from a Hebrew verb means "to live as a stranger," while the phrase translated as "an everlasting possession" means something permanent.³⁵ So, the possession of the land in the pre-587 era was temporary, and so not a fulfillment of the promise that they would have the land as an everlasting possession. Permanent possession still awaited them. The repetition in vv. 7 and 8 that Yhwh will be with Abraham and his descendants meant that "the divine presence" would be a guarantee of the promise of the land.³⁶

---

31. A more detailed treatment of the rise of Cyrus and the demise of Babylon will be found at the beginning of the next chapter.

32. There are two other Genesis texts that contain the promise of the land to Abraham: 12:1–9 and 15:1–21. At least 12:1–3 were known to the community in Babylon (Albertz, *Israel in Exile*, 252–55; Westermann, *Genesis 12–36*, 146–48).

33. Claus Westermann, *Genesis 12–36*, 225.

34. Westermann, *Genesis 12–36*, 262.

35. "To live as a stranger": גור; "the land of your sojourning": ארץ מגריך; "an everlasting possession": אחזת עולם. The precise meaning of the word אחזה ("possession") and its use in the P tradition is discussed by Bauks, "Die Begriffe."

36. The expression "divine presence" comes from Westermann, *Genesis 12–36*, 261.

The promise of descendants occurs again in vv. 17–22, where the focus is on Sarah's age and consequent infertility. She now becomes the recipient of Yhwh's favor: "your wife Sarah shall bear you a son, and you shall name him Isaac" (v. 19). The other major theme in the chapter is that of circumcision, which will be "the sign of the covenant between me and you" (v. 11).[37] The significance of Gen 17 for the exilic community is clear. They have a future: they will not diminish and die out. More importantly, cut off as they are from the visible symbol of Yhwh's presence in the Jerusalem temple, they are reassured that he is with them. This reassurance is the foundation then for the promise of permanent possession of the land.

Another ritual that P reinterpreted and developed for the community was Passover. P inherited a pre-Priestly text (Exod 12:21–23) and the Deuteronomic legislation about the feast.[38] Where 12:21–23 described Passover in apotropaic terms, serving to keep the angel of death away, P historicized it and connected directly to the deliverance from Egypt. Where Deut 16:1–7 sees Passover as a centralized feast "at the place that the LORD will choose as a dwelling place for his name" (v. 2), P's reinterpretation turns it into a household feast. The reinterpretation addressed the situation of the community in Babylon. Living in a foreign land, they were invited by the ritual into the world of the exodus generation in Egypt. The story of the exodus gave hope to those in Babylon, because it was a demonstration of Yhwh's power over the Egyptian deities, and showed them that his power was not confined to Judah or the Jerusalem temple, but was also at work in Babylon. So, just as the Israelites celebrated the Passover in Egypt in anticipation of their deliverance, so the exiles in Babylon could do likewise, as they also hoped for deliverance and a return to their homeland—"next year in Jerusalem."

Deutero-Isaiah: The Promised Deliverance

Prophecies about a future deliverance and a return to the land of Judah are also found in Isa 40–55. In wonderfully poetic, lyrical language, they highlight the incomparable power of Yhwh, and the promise of a glorious, triumphant return to the land.

---

37. The significance of circumcision for the exilic community is found earlier in this chapter, where I treat circumcision as an identity marker.
38. Abruyten, "Pollution-Purification Rituals," 137; Grünwaldt, *Exil und Identität*, 83.

THE COMMUNITY IN BABYLON AND THE EMERGENCE OF HOPE

Isaiah 40:1–11 is the prologue to chapters 40–55, and contains its great themes.[39] In these chapters, the theme of Israel's redemption is formulated against the backdrop of Deutero-Isaiah's understanding of Yhwh as the supreme deity and creator of the world. The theme of the sovereignty of Yhwh is then taken up in 40:12–31 in response to the exiles' questions about the impotence of Yhwh and the power of the Babylonian deities:

> Why do you say, O Jacob, and speak, O Israel,
> "My way is hidden from the LORD,
> and my right is disregarded by my God"? (v. 27)

The prophet then answers the complaint, declaring that Yhwh is incomparable, no deity can be compared to him (v. 18), he controls the destiny of nations (v. 15), and to him the inhabitants of the world are like grasshoppers (v. 22).[40]

The questions about Yhwh's power and the exiles' future are the subject of 44:24—45:8, which form part of the central section of chapters 40–48.[41] 44:24–28 begins with an affirmation of Yhwh's power as redeemer and the sole creator of the world (v. 24). Then in v. 25 he is portrayed as the one who confounds the Babylonian futurologists, while in v. 26a he validates "the word of his servant," a clear reference to the prophet/prophets we call Deutero-Isaiah and his/their message. Verses 25–26a address the doubts of those exiles still not convinced about the prophetic message addressed to them. Then vv. 26b and 28 reveal that Yhwh's plan for the future involves the rebuilding of Jerusalem, its temple, and the rest of Judah's cities. In v. 28 it is also revealed that Yhwh will bring about the promised future through the agency of Cyrus, the Persian emperor. He is called "my shepherd," and will "carry out all my purpose." Then the very next verse (45:1) reads "Thus says the LORD to his anointed, Cyrus." Calling Cyrus "my shepherd" and the "anointed one" would have shocked the audience because these terms were associated with the Davidic dynasty, and the only previous reference to a shepherd in chapters 40–55 was to Yhwh himself, the shepherd who would lead and care for his flock (40:11). However, simply using the terms "shepherd" and "anointed one" to designate Cyrus would hardly have

---

39. Baltzar summarizes them as: "God's sovereignty over the whole world, the election and redemption of Jacob/Israel, the renewal of Zion/Jerusalem, the dispute with foreign gods and their images, the revealing of the divine word" (Baltzar, *Deutero-Isaiah*, 47).

40. For more on the theme of the superiority of Yhwh, see Nilsen, "The Creation of Darkness and Evil (Isaiah 45:6c–7)."

41. So, Blenkinsopp, *Isaiah 40–55*, 245; Childs, *Isaiah*, 348–49.

quelled the doubters among the community about their future. So what follows in chapter 45 is another affirmation of Yhwh as the one and only God and creator (vv. 5–8 and 9–13). The mission of Cyrus is also described:

> I have aroused Cyrus in righteousness . . .
> he will build my city and set my exiles free. (v. 13)

The use of repeated rhetorical questions found in vv. 5–13 indicate a continued resistance on the part of the audience, and give us some insight into the struggle that they had in coming to accept the promised future and how it would be realized.

Other promises about a return to the land are found in chapter 51, where they are also underwritten by affirmations about Yhwh and his power as creator. 51:9–11 also contain a reference to the return to the land, expressed here in language that comes from Mesopotamian creation stories and also the exodus traditions:[42]

> Awake, awake, put on strength, O arm of the LORD!
> Awake, as in days of old, the generations of long ago!
> Is it not you who are cutting Rahab in pieces, piercing the dragon?
> Is it not you who dried up the sea, the waters of the great deep;
> who made the depths of the sea a way for the redeemed to cross over?
> So the ransomed of the LORD shall return, and come to Zion with singing;
> everlasting joy shall be upon their heads;
> they shall obtain joy and gladness,
> and sorrow and sighing shall flee away. (vv. 9–31)

As Ackroyd has noted, the verbs in vv. 10–11 are in the present tense, and so emphasize the here-and-now aspect of Yhwh's deliverance. The same Yhwh who created the world and brought Israel out of Egypt is now at work to bring about the return of the exiles to the homeland.[43]

The presence of exodus imagery is also central in chapter 52. The call to "comfort my people" in 40:1 is given a more concrete expression in 52:9: "The LORD has comforted his people, he has redeemed Jerusalem." Similarly, the image of the messenger of good news in 40:9 is repeated in 52:7. In the context of chapter 52, the comfort and the good news take the form of a departure from Babylon. Addressed to Jerusalem/Zion as a captive

---

42. Blenkinsopp, *Isaiah 40–55*, 332–33.

43. "The return of the exiles to Zion in rejoicing is the counterpart of the ransoming of the enslaved Israel and of the overthrow of the hostile forces of primeval chaos" (Ackroyd, *Exile and Restoration*, 130). For his comments about the translation of the verbs in 51:9–11, see Ackroyd, *Exile and Restoration*, 129.

daughter, the promise of deliverance is explicitly linked to the exodus: "Long ago, my people went down into Egypt to reside there as aliens" (v. 4). There is also an allusion to the departure from Egypt in v. 12. Unlike the departure from Egypt, which happened at short notice (Exod 12:33–34), leaving Babylon will not have the same urgency: "You shall not go out in haste, and you shall not go out in flight" (v. 12a). However, they will still have the same protection as did their ancestors when they left Egypt: "The LORD will go before you, and the God of Israel will be your rear guard" (v. 12b; cf. Exod 14:19).[44]

Besides using imagery from the exodus tradition, Deutero-Isaiah also makes use of the figure of Abraham in chapter 51. In 51:1–2 the exiles are reminded of their origins. Abraham and Sarah were their ancestors, the founders of the nation, and they had to make a similar journey to the promised land. The reference to them is compelling because they had no hope of children until Yhwh intervened. In the same way the exiles had no future without his intervention.[45]

Visions of the Future in Ezekiel

Just as the book of Ezekiel provided us with a radical reinterpretation of history in its condemnation of Judah, so its vision of the future is similarly radical. Although the first part of the book, chapters 1–24, is predominantly about judgment and punishment, it also contains short passages about a hope for the future. These are distinctive to Ezekiel, and are quite different to those we have seen in Isa 40–55. Ezekiel portrays the community in pre-587 Judah as corrupt and incapable of repentance. Before a future can be envisaged, the old corrupt order must be totally destroyed. So, in those parts of the book that are situated in the years before 587 the emphasis is on punishment and destruction. It is only when Jerusalem falls to the Babylonians that the book shifts focus and concentrates its attention on the possibility of a future for Israel. The Ezekiel texts have either minimal or no reference to the people's repentance or Yhwh's compassion as the foundation for the change in Yhwh's attitude from condemnation to deliverance. Ezekiel's emphasis is on the promised deliverance as a revelation of Yhwh to both Israel and the nations. He acts so that "they may know that I am the LORD" (e.g., 16:62; 17:24; 39:28).

44. Childs, *Exodus*, 406–7.
45. Childs, *Isaiah*, 402.

Ezekiel 1–24

The texts about the future hope are 11:14-21; 16:59-63; 17:22-24 and 20:40-44. Of these texts 11:14-21 is the most extensive in its representation of the future.

11:14-21 are part of a major unit of text, chapters 8–11, which describe abominations being carried out in the temple (8:6-17), a vision of Yhwh's punishment (chapter 9), and a description of Yhwh's withdrawal from the temple (chapter 10). The themes of judgment and punishment are continued in 11:1-13, but then comes a radical shift. What comes next in 11:14-21 are the first words in the book that promise deliverance for the exiles.

They are introduced by a quotation from a taunt by the inhabitants of Jerusalem directed against the exiles in Babylon: "They have gone far from the LORD; to us this land is given for a possession" (v. 15). The point of the taunt in v. 15 is that those in Jerusalem who survived the Babylonian invasion regarded themselves as the rightful owners of the land, while the exiles had forfeited their rights in this matter. Verses 16-21 is Yhwh's response. The first point in the response is an affirmation that, although the exiles "had been removed far away among the nations" (v. 16), Yhwh was still with them as a "sanctuary to some extent" (v. 16).[46] In other words, even though the exiles were outside the land and far from the temple, they still had a relationship with him.

Verse 17 then promises that Yhwh will gather all those scattered outside of Judah and return them to the land. However, the return is only one element in Ezekiel's vision of their future. Yhwh then promises that he will radically transform the exiles by giving them a new spirit and an undivided heart, so that they can again enter into a covenant with him (vv. 19-20). Yhwh's initiative was necessary to bring about a future for them because up to this moment their hearts were so corrupt that they were incapable of obeying his commandments.[47] The exiles then would live in the land as a transformed and renewed people. The promise of a future in 11:14-21

---

46. A "sanctuary to some extent" is the translation suggested by Joyce, *Ezekiel*, 113. The meaning of the Hebrew expression למקדש מעט in v. 9 has been much debated. For further see Hiebel, *Ezekiel's Vision Accounts*, 303-4; Joyce, *Ezekiel*, 113-14.

47. For a good explanation of the meaning of "heart" and "spirit" in this context, see Joyce, *Ezekiel*, 114-16. On the transformation of the people, see also Hiebel, *Ezekiel's Vision Accounts*, 137-38.

THE COMMUNITY IN BABYLON AND THE EMERGENCE OF HOPE

does not embrace those who are still in Jerusalem. Their fate, as vv. 1–13 indicate, will be death and the destruction of their land.[48]

The exiles of 597 are also looked on favorably in chapter 17, which again reflects a tension between the two communities.[49] Chapter 17 contains an allegory about the Babylonian conquest of 597, when Nebuchadnezzar took king Jehoiachin as a prisoner to Babylon and put Zedekiah on the throne in Judah (vv. 10). As the interpretation of the allegory makes clear, Zedekiah will be punished by death because of his rebellion against the Babylonians (vv. 12–21). In contrast, vv. 22–24 portray a hopeful future for Jehoiachin. He is portrayed as the twig of a cedar tree planted on a high mountain. When it is fully grown all kinds of birds will shelter in its shade (v. 23). According to vv. 17–24 then, Israel's future will also include leadership by a descendant of Jehoiachin.

There are also visions of the future in 16:59–63 and 20:40–44, but they have an unusual character. Even though they both speak of a future for Israel, there is almost a resentment in Yhwh's promise. As we have seen earlier, chapter 16 presents a bleak and extremely negative portrait of the people, portraying them as a shameless prostitute.[50] It concludes in v. 58 with the warning, "You must bear the penalty of your lewdness and your abominations, says the LORD." This negative tone continues in v. 59 with the threat: "I will deal with you as you have done, you who have despised the oath, breaking my covenant." The tone of v. 59 suggests that what follows should logically be something like a prophetic judgment speech, or an announcement of some impending disaster. Instead there is the opposite. Verse 62 is the announcement that Yhwh will enter into a covenant with the people. Then there is another unexpected twist in v. 63. Often texts that announce a covenant between Yhwh and Israel like v. 62 will say something like "And you shall be my people, and I will be your God," and that the past will not be brought to mind.[51] Instead, according to v. 63, Yhwh's purpose in entering into a covenant relationship is to shame and confound Israel,

---

48. Allen, *Ezekiel 1–19*, 165–66. On the tension between the two groups, see Rom-Shiloni, "Ezekiel," 11–18.

49. For further on chapter 17, see commentaries such as Allen, *Ezekiel 1–19*, 256–62; Joyce, *Ezekiel*, 136–37.

50. See pages 34–36 earlier.

51. E.g., Gen 9:9–11; Jer 31:33–34.

CONSTRUCTING EXILE

and reduce it to silence. It is almost a vindictive action by Yhwh. It may be a covenant of grace, but is certainly not one of graciousness and compassion.[52]

In v. 62 we find what is often called the recognition formula: "you shall know that I am the LORD." Found in other places in Ezekiel, in texts about either judgment or deliverance, its use is intended to focus our attention primarily on Yhwh and what he has done, and not on the condition or attitude of the people. The presence of the recognition formula in 15:62 reinforces the theocentric view of the book of Ezekiel, in which "the focus is upon the God who is known rather than upon those by whom he is known"[53] In 16:59-63, and in the other texts, which are treated next, Israel is a figure that is firstly admonished, and only then promised a future. Any action of Israel, whether knowing Yhwh or repenting, is totally dependent of Yhwh's initiative.[54]

The vision of the future in 20:40-44 is similar to that in 16:59-63, except that it has a less abrasive character. Chapter 20, as we have seen earlier, portrays Israel's history as one of corruption and infidelity to Yhwh from its beginning.[55] It concludes its historical retrospective with the rather startling command to Israel; "Go serve your idols, everyone of you now and hereafter" (v. 34). As with chapter 16, we would expect some words of judgment or a threat of punishment to follow such a command. Instead there is an abrupt shift in attitude in v. 40: "All the house of Israel, all of them, shall serve me in the land." Then the people will be gathered from all the places where they have been scattered by Yhwh. By this action the holiness of his name will be revealed the nations (v. 41). Then in the land, they will be confronted with their infidelity, and be reduced almost to a state of self-hatred: "You shall loathe yourselves for all the evils that you have committed" (v. 43). However, as a result of the confrontation they will know "that I am the LORD" (v. 44). Again, as in 16:59-63, the foundation for Yhwh's deliverance is not the positive disposition of Israel, but the revelation of his holiness to the nations.

---

52. As Zimmerli writes, "this promise for Jerusalem's future does not mean a superficial and hasty glossing over of the past . . . but that a shameful memory will remain alive" (Zimmerli, *Ezekiel 1*, 353).

53. Joyce, *Divine Initiative*, 94. The use of the formula in Ezekiel is treated extensively by Zimmerli, *I Am Yahweh*, 29-98.

54. For further see Joyce, *Divine Initiative*, 93-95.

55. See pages 37-38 earlier.

THE COMMUNITY IN BABYLON AND THE EMERGENCE OF HOPE

Ezekiel 33-37

The visions of a hopeful future, concentrated in chapters 34-37, are preceded by 33:23-29, which mark the major turning point in the book.[56] 33:1-20 recapitulate much of chapters 1-24 and Ezekiel's ministry of warning the people of Yhwh's impending punishment, and their resistance to his message. 33:20, the last verse before the book's turning point, reflects the people's inability to accept responsibility for their situation: "Yet you say, 'The way of the LORD is not just'" (v. 20).[57] Verses 23-39 introduce the new era, which begins with the capture of Jerusalem by the Babylonians in 587 (v. 21):

> In the twelfth year of our exile, in the tenth month, on the fifth day of the month, someone who had escaped from Jerusalem came to me and said, "The city has fallen." (33:21)

From this point on the book is dominated by hopeful visions of the future, which include a return to the land and the building of a new temple. The future is not brought about by Israel's repentance, but rather by the initiative of Yhwh. However, there could be no future until the hopelessly comprised and defiled present had been wiped out. Into this spiritual vacuum Yhwh speaks his words of deliverance.

The first text containing a vision of hope for the future is found in chapter 34. The context is the prophetic condemnation of Judah's leaders, specifically their kings.[58] Portrayed as shepherds they are denounced by Yhwh for neglecting their sheep and looking after themselves: "My shepherds have not searched for my sheep, but the shepherds have fed themselves, and have not fed my sheep" (v. 8). Visions of the future are found in vv. 9-16 and vv. 20-31. In vv. 9-16 Yhwh takes over as the true shepherd of the people, whom he will rescue from wherever they have been scattered, bring them back to their land, and provide excellent pasture for them (vv. 13-14). In vv. 20-31 the content of the vision is modified. The imagery of shepherd and sheep is maintained, but the new shepherd will not be Yhwh but a Davidic descendant ("my servant David"—v. 23). In the promised future Yhwh will enter into a covenant of peace with the people. There will also be a restoration of the land. The ravages of war will be removed

---

56. So, Joyce, *Ezekiel*, 190.

57. Joyce, *Ezekiel*, 192-93.

58. Joyce, *Ezekiel*, 196. For an over view of chapter 34, see Klein, "Salvation for Sheep and Bones."

and fertility restored, so that Israel will have the guarantee of a secure source of food (vv. 26–29).[59] The existence of the covenant is reaffirmed in v. 30, and the chapter concludes with declaration that Yhwh is the shepherd of the sheep, a statement that stands in tension with the earlier reference in v. 23 to a Davidic shepherd. Overall, the book of Ezekiel does not have any enthusiasm for a return of the Davidic dynasty, so in v. 23 the future Davidic shepherd is not referred to as a king, but simply as a prince.[60] As seen earlier, the end result of Yhwh's action is again that the people will acknowledge him as their God (vv. 30–31).

The next Ezekiel text about the vision of the future is chapter 36, which divides into three sections, vv. 1–15, 16–32, and 33–38. The oracle in vv. 1–15 is addressed to "the mountains of Israel" (v. 1), which stand for the whole land. It declares a transformation of the land and its "desolate wastes" and "deserted towns" (v. 3), which were the result of Yhwh's punishment for the abominations committed by its inhabitants. The land will become fertile, its population of people and animals increased, and it will experience an abundance of Yhwh's blessings: "I will cause you to be inhabited as in former times, and will do more good to you than ever before" (v. 11).

The vision of the future in 36:16–32 is rather different. It consists of a review of Israel's sinful past (vv. 17–21) followed by an announcement of deliverance (vv. 17–32). The language of defilement is used to describe the sinful past. The people's behavior was like the uncleanness of a menstruating woman (v. 17), because their worship of idols defiled the land (v. 18). As a result, they were banished from there and scattered in different countries (v. 19). The announcement of deliverance that follows has some unusual characteristics, which are unique to Ezekiel. According to v. 20, when Israel was scattered among the different nations, they still profaned Yhwh's "holy name." However, the profaning did not result from their behavior, but rather from the fact that they were in some way an affront or embarrassment to Yhwh, because "it was said of them, 'These are the people of the LORD, and yet they had to go out of his land'" (v. 20). Then as vv. 21–22 explain, the motivation for Yhwh's promise to bring them back to the land is not his compassion for them, but rather is "for the sake of my holy name which you have profaned among the nations to which you came" (v. 22). The result of Yhwh's action will be not only the return to the land but also the total

---

59. One of the outcomes of invasion is the destruction of agricultural land, and the consequent lack of food for the survivors. For further, see Kelle, "Trauma of Defeat."

60. In v. 23 the MT has נשׂיא ("prince"), not מלך ("king").

transformation of the people. Again portrayed as hopelessly corrupt, incapable of doing good, a people whose origins and whole history were sinful, they will be transformed by the gift of a new heart and a new spirit (v. 26). Restored to the land of their ancestors, they will again be Yhwh's covenant partner (v. 28). They have a future not because they deserved it but because Yhwh has determined it.[61]

Ezekiel's vision of the dry bones (37:1–14), one of the best-known parts of the book, is also a vision of the future. The bones represent Israel in exile, who complain that they are a people without hope (v. 11).[62] As a nation the people are dead (and, according to v. 12, buried). 37:1–14 links back to chapters 8–11, which portrays Jerusalem as filled with the dead bodies of those killed by Yhwh's executioners.[63] Now, Yhwh promises that his people will be brought back to life. The revival consists of two phases. The first is in vv. 4–8, in which the bones receive sinews, flesh, and skin, but as yet they do not have life. The second phase is in vv. 9–10, in which the bones receive the breath of life, "and they lived and stood on their feet, a vast multitude" (v. 10). In vv. 11–14, which spell out the meaning of the vision, there is a further development in Israel's resuscitation. There is a promise of a return to the land in v. 12, a journey from a place of death to one of new life.[64] They will also receive the gift of a new spirit, that of Yhwh himself, and as a result they will realize that their future is the work of Yhwh alone: "You shall know that I am the LORD" (vv. 13, 14).

The final aspect of the vision for the future in chapter 37 is the reunification of Judah and Israel (vv. 15–28). Ezekiel is commanded to take two sticks, representing Judah and Israel, and to join them together in his hand. The symbolic act is then explained as not just the reunion of Judah and Israel, but as symbolizing a new identity as a cleansed and renewed people, who have been brought back to their homeland, and are once again covenant partners with Yhwh (v. 23). They will again live under the rule of

---

61. "In the use of a range of formulae and motifs in Ezekiel we find evidence of a distinctive emphasis on the absolute centrality of Yhwh and his self-manifestation, a radical theocentricity that is of an order difficult to parallel anywhere in the Hebrew Bible" (Joyce, *Ezekiel*, 27).

62. Verse 11 refers to the people as being "cut off," but it is not clear from what. Joyce has suggested that the complaint is possibly a quote from a well-known dirge (Joyce, *Ezekiel*, 209).

63. Hiebel, "Visions," 245–48.

64. Hiebel puts it well when she writes "the vast multitude . . . finally has received it marching orders" (Hiebel, *Ezekiel's Vision Accounts*, 161).

a Davidic descendant, who is described as both shepherd and king (v. 24). In v. 25 however, the future Davidic ruler is not called a king, but rather a prince, the same designation as found in chapter 34 and its vision of the future.[65] The book's ambiguity about a future Davidic leader is reflected not only in chapters 34 and 37, but also in what follows, the great vision of the future temple in chapters 40–48.

Ezekiel 40–48

Ezekiel 40–48 concludes the book with an extensive vision of the future. 40:1 situates it in the year 572. The prophet's vision is of a new temple filled with the glory of Yhwh, and of the land systematically divided among the twelve tribes.[66] The future temple is described in 40:5—42:20. Here Ezekiel is given a guided tour by an anonymous and mysterious figure: "a man was there, whose appearance shone like bronze, with a linen cord and measuring reed in his hand" (40:3). The temple's structure, especially the walls and gates, are described in detail in 40:5—42:20. Its basic ground plan shows the building divided into three areas of increasing holiness: the outer court, the inner court, and the "most holy place" (NRSV), often referred to as the "holy of holies."

The centrepiece of chapters 40–48 is 43:1–12, the account of Yhwh's return. Having departed from the old Jerusalem temple because of the abominations committed there and settled in Babylon (chapters 8–11), the glory of Yhwh returned and entered the temple by the east gate, went into the holy of holies, and filled the temple (43:5). In v. 7 Yhwh begins to speak to Ezekiel, and recalls Israel's past abominations. Again we encounter the theme of Israel's shame, and again in the context of the vision of the future (43:8–12; also 44:6–14). The memory of Israel's sinful past will always be held up before the people, even in a text that portrays a future in such positive, utopian terms (43:8–12).

The next significant element in the vision are the regulations about worship (chapter 44), and the plan for a radical redistribution of the land

---

65. As noted by Joyce, *Ezekiel*, 211. For further on the significance of the two terms in this context, see Tuell, "Divine Presence and Absence," 104. The tension about the Davidic character of the future ruler may reflect a later redactional insertion (so, e.g., Klein, "Salvation for Sheep and Bones," 184–85).

66. For an overview of chapters 40–48, see Stevenson, *The Vision of Transformation*, 143–65. On the Babylonian background of chapters 40–48, see Leveen, "Returning the Body," 388–90.

THE COMMUNITY IN BABYLON AND THE EMERGENCE OF HOPE

among the former twelve tribes (45:1–8), which is then taken up and expanded in chapter 48. Each of the tribes was to receive an equal share of land, as was the prince (48:21), in a vision that "reflects an idealized picture of a pre-monarchic egalitarian society."[67]

The utopian vision about the allotment of land touches on the question about the purpose not just of chapter 48 but of the whole of chapters 40–48. Are they *a real blueprint* for a new Jerusalem temple, the description of a heavenly temple to be built by Yhwh, or a vision of *a utopian future* that looks beyond the horizon of history to the end time,? On balance the latter is the more likely possibility.[68] The temple and the allotment of land described in chapters 40–48 have some unusual features. There is no role given to a king in the new temple. Rather there are references to a prince (נשיא) in 43:3 and 46:2–18 in which his access to the temple and cultic role is tightly controlled. There is no explicit reference to the ruler being a Davidic descendant.[69] As Albertz notes, a future king would have no official cultic role, but would be "simply the most distinguished representative of the lay community."[70]

Another unusual characteristic of the future temple is its location. It is not situated in a city but in the land allotted to the Zadokite priests (48:8, 21). Unlike the temple of Solomon, the new temple is separated from the monarchy, just like the new city. According to 48:35 the name of the new city is "Yhwh is there." While the reference to the high mountain in 40:2 might be an allusion to Jerusalem and the Zion theology, it is striking that neither are mentioned in the whole of chapters 40–48. These omissions would support the view that chapters 40–48 are not a blueprint for a rebuilding program, but a vision of an idealized future. There are, however, a couple references to something that did actually become part of the community's self-identity, both in Babylon and in later times. This was the idea of separation. In 42:20 we read of the wall around the temple whose function was "to make a separation between the holy and the common."

---

67. Albertz, *Israel in Exile*, 373. See also Stevenson, *The Vision of Transformation*, 157–58.

68. On the different views of various scholars, see e.g., Leveen, "Returning the Body," 386 n.3; Joyce, *Ezekiel*, 220–21; Stevenson, *The Vision of Transformation*, 149–51; Tuell, "Ezekiel 40–42 as Verbal Icon"; Stevenson, *The Vision of Transformation*, 149–51.

69. For a discussion on the identity of the prince in chapters 40–48, see Stevenson, *The Vision of Transformation*, 119–23. On the references to David, see Sedlmeier, "The Figure of David."

70. Albertz, *Israel in Exile*, 372.

44:5, 9 then addresses the issue of who may be admitted to the temple and who is to be excluded. In this respect the vision shares a similarity with the Priestly tradition and its vision of the future, which was described earlier in this chapter.[71]

Summary—Visions of the Future in Ezekiel

Visions of the future are found in the sections of the book that are about both judgment and deliverance. In the first part of the book, chapters 1–24, they are only a few verses long and occur in the context of the prophet's denouncements of the people. In chapters 33–37 and 40–48 they occur in texts that almost exclusively refer to future deliverance.

There are some common themes in the visions found both in chapters 1–24 and 33–37. One is the motivation for Yhwh's promise of deliverance. Unlike in Isaiah or Jeremiah, where the motive is Yhwh's compassion for his people, in Ezekiel the motivation is that the deliverance of his people will reveal to both Israel and the surrounding nations that "I am the LORD." The focus is squarely on Yhwh, and not on the people's disposition. Another theme is that the deliverance will result in a transformation of the people. Ezekiel routinely portrays them as corrupt and incapable of doing good. Yhwh's deliverance involves bringing them back to the land, and entering into a new covenant relationship with them. A further feature is a renewed leadership. In place of the shepherds who led the flock astray, Yhwh will become their new shepherd and will not abandon the flock. A future Davidic ruler figures in some of the texts about the future, but the book reveals an ambiguity about the future of the Davidic dynasty. Where there is reference to a future Davidic leader, he is referred to not as a king but as a prince.

The book concludes with the utopian vision of a new temple and a radical redistribution of the land (chapters 40–48). The glory of Yhwh, which departed from the temple in chapters 8–11, returns to the holy of holies. The Zadokite priests have a central role in the new temple's worship, whereas there is no such role given to a future Davidic rule. In the vision of the new temple there is no reference to Jerusalem or the restoration of its temple. The new temple is situated within a city, whose name is only revealed at the very end of the book: "The name of the city henceforth shall be: Yhwh is there" (48:35).

---

71. Pages 49–50.

THE COMMUNITY IN BABYLON AND THE EMERGENCE OF HOPE

From the point of view of the book of Ezekiel, there could be no talk of a future until the sinful and corrupt past—i.e., pre-587 Judah—was destroyed. The future that the book portrays is of a completely new order. To that extent it is utopian, and, as we shall see, it was never realized.

SUMMARY

The focus in this chapter has been on the exiles, their situation in Babylon, and the question of their future. The chapter has shown how they responded to the crisis brought about by the demise of Judah and their forced migration to Babylon. Responses to the crisis were not uniform. There is evidence that some assimilated into the local culture, and the denunciation of idol worship in Deutero-Isaiah suggests that some adopted the local religion. However, among other circles a belief emerged that they had a future.

One element of the belief was that they saw themselves as a community that was clearly distinct from the surrounding culture. A sense of identity was constructed by the P theologians, who looked back at some of the traditions of pre-587 Judah and reinterpreted these for their situation in Babylon. Sabbath observance, circumcision, and dietary laws became identity markers for the exiles. They also saw themselves as the inheritors of the promises made to Abraham and his descendants that the land of Canaan would be theirs not as a place of sojourning, but as an everlasting possession.

In Deutero-Isaiah and the book of Ezekiel grand and utopian visions of the future were promised. According to Deutero-Isaiah, the exiles would be led back to Judah in an even more wondrous way than their ancestors were brought out of Egypt and into the promised land. According to the book of Ezekiel, they would be brought back to the land and recreated as a people, covenant partners with Yhwh. There would be a new distribution of land, and a new temple in which the glory of Yhwh would be present. There would also be a new city, not called Jerusalem, but "Yhwh is there."

What we have seen in this chapter are visions of the future, not actual realities. Our next step is to see if the visions were ever realized. Or, in other words, was there an end to the exile, and was there a restoration?

Chapter 5

THE EARLY PERSIAN PERIOD
From Exile to Restoration?

BABYLONIAN DOMINATION ENDED WITH the rise of the Persians under Cyrus. In this chapter we study the situation of the Judahite communities in Babylon and Judah, and see what impact the Persian conquest had on them. Did it mean that there was an end to their exile in Babylon, and did they return home? Was there a rebuilding of the community and its infrastructure in Judah? Or, to frame the questions another way: was there an end to exile, and a restoration in Judah?

To answer these questions, we will first review the historical situation in both Babylon and Judah in the aftermath of the Persian conquest. Then we will look at texts that either narrate or make predictions about life in Yehud in the early Persian period. We will see that the texts portray exile and its significance differently, and do likewise with the idea of a restoration. As will become clear, exile, especially in the book of Ezra, and restoration are not just historical events but also literary constructions that advance the theological claims of particular groups within the Judahite community. In contrast, the book of Haggai does not mention either exile or exiles at all.

THE RISE OF CYRUS: THE DEMISE OF BABYLON

Nebuchadnezzar died in 562. From this point on Babylonian power was on the wane. There were four rulers in a period of six years. The one who held power for the longest was Nabonidus, who took power in 556. Against this background of instability, the empire started to disintegrate. In 553, the year after the death of Nabonidus, Cyrus II led a Persian rebellion against the Medes, the people who were neighbors to the Persians but had sided with the Babylonians. In 546 Cyrus became ruler of Persia and Media. He began a program of expansion that included the conquest of Babylon in 539. What was Judah now became Yehud, a province of the Persian Empire, and an area of land smaller than the pre-exilic former southern kingdom.

The Persians in general, and Cyrus in particular, have been regarded as more tolerant of conquered peoples' way of life than were the Babylonians. The Cyrus Cylinder has often been quoted as the source for this understanding.[1] However, it has its own agenda of advancing the reputation of Cyrus, and therefore needs to be critically interpreted.[2] According to the Cylinder, the conquest of Babylon by Cyrus had two causes. One was that Nabonidus had removed the god Marduk from his place of prominence, thus displeasing him and earning divine retribution. The second was that Marduk then chose Cyrus as his favored servant: "then he pronounced the name of Cyrus, king of Anshan, declared him to become ruler of all the world."[3] Under the protection and guidance of Marduk, Cyrus was able to conquer Babylon without bloodshed:

> Because Marduk . . . was pleased with Cyrus' good deeds and upright heart, he ordered him to march against Babylon.[4]

According to the cylinder, he was welcomed by the priests of Marduk, but in reality it was rather that Cyrus had organized them to hail him as the city's liberator.[5] As Briant writes, "This traditional interpretation evokes suspicion to the extent that it agrees with the image that Persian propaganda itself would have portrayed."[6]

---

1. The Cyrus Cylinder, housed in the British Museum, is a cuneiform text written on a tablet shaped in the form of a cylinder. It presents Cyrus as a model ruler.

2. Briant refers to the sources such as the cylinder as being "one-sided" (Briant, *From Cyrus to Alexander*, 40).

3. Pritchard, *ANET*, 315, line 12.

4. Pritchard, *ANET*, 315, lines 11–12. The manner by which Cyrus conquered the well-fortified city of Babylon has been much discussed by historians. For details of the discussion, see Vanderhooft, "Cyrus II."

5. Albertz, *Israel in Exile*, 70.

6. Briant, *From Cyrus to Alexander*, 41.

At his death in 530, Cyrus was succeeded by his son Cambyses, who ruled until he died in 522. At this point the empire was hopelessly overextended and began to tear itself apart internally.[7] Out of the chaos Darius emerged as emperor in 522. The revolt and unrest continued until around 519 when Darius was able to institute a period of stability. In the years that followed he reformed the administrative structure and introduced a new system of government and taxation. Persian policy was to strengthen the local regimes to use them to support the empire, and "to use the resources of the empire to support politically important regions."[8] Political expediency rather than religious devotion was the reason for the Achaemenids to allow and support the continued existence of conquered peoples' cults.[9] It is against that background that we now examine the significance of the Persian conquest, and its impact on both the community of deportees and their descendants in Babylon, and on those who remained in Judah.

UNDER PERSIAN RULE

There are two sections under this heading. The first is to determine the significance of the Persian conquest for the community in Babylon. The second is to see its significance for Yehud.

The Community in Babylon

We first need to appreciate that the Judean population in Babylon ("the exiles") was not a monolithic group, but consisted of: a) those who saw themselves as a distinctive group faithful to Yhwh; b) those who had economically integrated into Babylonian society but maintained their Yahwistic faith; c) those who abandoned their ancestral religion and took on that of the Babylonians. Of these groups, the biblical texts would indicate that the first would have been most affected by the change from Babylonian to Persian oversight. For them the triumph of Cyrus would have made possible the return to Judah that was promised in Isa 40–55. However, the picture is not so simple. By 539, the year that Cyrus occupied Babylon,

---

7. Blenkinsopp, *Ezra-Nehemiah*, 77, 96.
8. Albertz, *Israel in Exile*, 119.
9. The Achaemenid policy is discussed at length by Bedford, *Temple Restoration*, 133–49.

the Judahite community consisted of people exiled in 597, 587, and 582, together with their descendants. What we do not know is how many of those exiles were still alive, and how would they have survived the rigors of the long journey to Yehud. We also do not know the attitude of their descendants. Born in Babylon, did they see it or Judah as their homeland? Did they think of themselves as exiles?

The second group are those who integrated themselves into the economic structures of Babylon. We do not know whether this came about because they followed the advice of Jeremiah (Jer 29:4–9) to think of Babylon as their real home, as Jerusalem once was. Their integration may have been made purely on economic grounds. The presence of Yahwistic names in the Yahudu tablets could possibly indicate that they maintained their ancestral religion, as a colony of Assyrians were able to do in Babylon.[10] Integrated then into the local society, they would hardly have seen themselves as exiles, or at least came to believe that they could still be followers of Yhwh while living in a foreign "promised land."

The Community in Yehud

The demise of Babylon and the rise of Persia meant that Judah was still under foreign occupation. It was now a small part of a massive empire that at its peak spread from Egypt to modern-day India. The empire had a strong central government and good communications. The reorganization of Darius in 520 added to it an efficient administration and taxation system. There were military and trade routes through Syria-Palestine, and these were protected by the Persian military. Yehud was strategically important, because it was a border state lying next to Egypt. For the Persians the security and stability of Yehud was an important factor in their larger political ambition to control and possibly invade Egypt, so the inhabitants of Yehud would have been very familiar with the presence of the Persian military in the area.[11] While biblical texts such as Ezra and Nehemiah might give the impression that Yehud had a special standing in the eyes of the Persian administration, it was still the latter that was in control of the political

---

10. On the Assyrians and their worship in Babylon of the deity Ahhur see Beaulieu, "Yahwistic Names," 254–55.

11. Briant, *From Cyrus to Alexander*, 48.

situation and not the former.[12] Any favorable treatment of Yehud by the Persians has to be interpreted in this context.[13]

In 535 Cyrus incorporated what was Judah and all of Syria-Palestine west of the Euphrates river into a single province, and installed an Iranian named Gubaru as its governor.[14] In 520 the area west of the Euphrates was established as the district of "Across the River."[15]

Under the Persians the population of Yehud grew, initially only gradually. Judah had suffered extensive damage during the during the Babylonian conquest and occupation. Its pre-587 population was estimated at between 110,000 and 140,000. In the early Persian period, its population was about 13,000, but may have reached 30,000 by the fifth century BCE.[16]

Jerusalem was substantially destroyed. Its settled area was diminished by about 90 percent, and was possibly uninhabited during the Babylonian era.[17] In the early sixth century Mizpah grew in size, becoming the administrative center after 587.[18] It continued to be such until sometime in the fifth century when Jerusalem regained its position as the capital.[19] Although limited in resources compared to pre-587 Judah, Yehud was still able to produce written texts that later became part of the Hebrew scriptures. The book of Lamentations took shape in post-587 Judah, as did the later redactions of the Deuteronomistic history.[20] Besides Jerusalem, Mizpah was a

---

12. Gerstenberger, *Israel in the Persian Period*, 86. Issues about the historicity of Ezra and Nehemiah are taken up below, pages 78–81.

13. Regarding favors granted by Persian emperors, Briant writes: "Resituated in the ideological and political context of the Near East, they again become what they had been originally: certainly an important episode for the Jews themselves, but a banal and typical event that many Near Eastern people would already have experienced in the course of Assyrian and Babylonian dominion" (Briant, *From Cyrus to Alexander*, 48). An extended treatment of the period is given by Gerstenberger, *Israel in the Persian Period*, 45–117.

14. Dandamayev, "Neo-Babylonian and Achaemenid State Administration in Mesopotamia," 376 See also Betylon, "Palestine," 6.

15. Lipschits, "Achaemenid Imperial Policy," 25.

16. Becking, "We All Returned as One," 7. A figure of 30,000 is given by Lipschits, "Demographic Changes," 364. His calculations are based on a larger Yehud than Becking's, and come from a later time in Persian period (Becking, "We All Returned as One," 9 n.16).

17. See earlier in chapter 2 for this information and its sources.

18. Lipschits, "Demographic Changes," 347 A detailed discussion of the archaeological evidence about Mizpah and its significance is given by Zorn, "Tell en-Naṣbeh," 433–43.

19. Lemaire, "Nabonidus," 292.

20. Albertz, *Israel in Exile*, 130.

possible center for such activity because it was the place where Gedaliah, the Babylonian appointed administrator of post-587 Judah, was located.[21] He was a descendant of Shaphan, the court scribe of Josiah, and an advocate of the Deuteronomistic reforms. The Shaphan family were also protectors of Jeremiah (Jer 26:24; 39:14; 40:5). In the aftermath of 587 and his release from prison, Jeremiah was placed in the care of Gedaliah at Mizpah. Here the pre-Masoretic text of the book of Jeremiah took shape.[22]

Exile and Diaspora

As we saw earlier, the Babylonian invasion caused people from Judah to disperse into various surrounding countries. The book of Ezekiel used the word "exile" and "exiles" to refer only to the deportees in Babylon. Others who left Judah as a result of the invasions are referred to as either "scattered" or "dispersed"—i.e., in diaspora. So, exile in Babylon, especially when referred to as "*the* exile" represents the experience of only a segment of the Judahite population. In the early Persian period we can also identify several other groups of Judahites living outside their homeland.[23] The book of Jeremiah in several places refers to those who had escaped the Babylonian invasion of 597 by going to Egypt (24:8; chapters 43-44).[24] The command in 43:18 that Jeremiah perform a prophetic action at the entrance of Pharaoh's palace suggests that the Judahites in Egypt were neither a small group nor latecomers.[25] There was also the colony of Judahitess at Elephantine, an island in the river Nile. It was a fort set up by mercenaries, among whom were Judahites.[26] While the settlement began, possibly as early as 650, documentary evidence establishes that by 525 they had built their own temple dedicated to Yhwh.[27] The inhabitants of the colony showed no concern about remaining in Elephantine, despite some mistreatment by the local population and the decree of Cyrus, which allowed people to go up to Jerusalem to rebuild the temple (Ezra 1:3).[28]

21. On Jerusalem as the site for scribal activity, see Ben Zvi, "Yehud," 46.
22. Hill, "Writing the Prophetic Word."
23. A list similar to what follows is given by Kessler, "Diaspora and Homeland," 141.
24. On the community in Egypt, see Albertz, *Israel in Exile*, 96-97.
25. B. Porten, *Archives from Elephantine*, 14.
26. Fried, *The Priest and the Great King*, 93.
27. The date of 650 is proposed by Bezalel Porten, "Settlement," 461.
28. Albertz, *Israel in Exile*, 97-98; Talmon, "'Exile' and 'Restoration,'" 120-21.

So, by the early Persian period, Judahites did not exist *only* in the bipolar communities of those in Yehud and the exiles in Babylon. It is also an oversimplification to think that all those living outside Yehud saw themselves as exiles and as longing to return to the homeland. Even in texts from Ezra, which is so focussed on a return from exile, there is no censure against those who remained in Babylon. Similarly, when Nehemiah asked the Persian ruler if he could go to Jerusalem, he did not ask to emigrate.[29] When the temple-dedication prayer of Solomon refers to people outside the land praying "towards their land" (1 Kgs 8:48), it does not promise a return to the land, but simply that their captors may show them compassion. First Kings 8:45–33 "points to a time in which the exiles accepted their fate and started to live in foreign lands."[30] In the aftermath of the Babylonian era, Judahites became a "multicentric" people.[31] While diaspora might more accurately describe their situation, we will see below that others understood themselves as "exiles" and attached a particular theological or ideological significance to the word.

EXILE AND RESTORATION IN HAGGAI AND ZECHARIAH 1–8

Although the book of Ezra purports to describe the return of exiles soon after Cyrus' conquest of Babylon, it originated in a later time. The books of Haggai and Zech 1–8 are earlier compositions, and so give us a very different account of events that happened soon after 539, whereas the books of Ezra and Nehemiah reflect the conflicts of the fifth or fourth centuries BCE. So, we begin with Haggai and Zech 1–8.

The Book of Haggai

The book of Haggai, only two chapters long, covers a three-month period in the year 520, and is the best biblical witness we have to the early years of

---

29. So, Knoppers, "Construction," 2.

30. Fritz, *1 & 2 Kings*, 100. For 1 Kgs 8:46–51 as text originating in the "late exilic" or "early post-exilic" period after the rebuilding of the temple, see e.g., Knoppers, "Prayer and Propaganda," 389; O'Brien, *The Deuteronomistic History Hypothesis*, 284.

31. Talmon describes the shift that happened in the early Persian period as a movement from "monocentricity" to "multicentricity" (Talmon, "'Exile' and 'Restoration,'" 129).

THE EARLY PERSIAN PERIOD

the Persian occupation of Yehud.[32] It has no specific references to the exile in Babylon, but only some indirect allusions. It is concerned with restoration, and specifically with two aspects—the rebuilding of the Jerusalem temple and the promise of a Davidic ruler for Judah.

Haggai 1:1 provides the setting for the book. The word of Yhwh comes to Haggai "in the second year of king Darius, in the sixth month, on the first day of the month." This is the year 520. The book assumes the existence of a functioning community in Yehud by that time and that this community had been there for an unspecified period. It had a governor, Zerubbabel, appointed by the Persians, and a high priest, Joshua. At the time the community was in a situation of distress and hardship, suffering poor harvests, drought, hunger, and poverty. The Jerusalem temple was in ruins, but the book makes no reference about when or why it was destroyed. The community was in conflict over its rebuilding, as chapter 1 indicates. Haggai 1:2 quotes unnamed people who "say the time has not yet come to rebuild the LORD's house." No reason is given for their stance. Haggai then pointed to their current economic woes as Yhwh's punishment for their inaction (1:4–12). He also accused them of living in houses that were in better condition than the remains of the Jerusalem temple (1:4). The people responded positively to the prophet's message and went to work on the rebuilding.

What then does the book of Haggai tell us about exile and restoration? There is no mention of the word "exile" or "exiles" in the book, and no reference to a diaspora.[33] When Haggai confronts the community about their delay in rebuilding the temple, he simply calls them "these people" (1:2). Later in the book, they are referred to as a "remnant" (1:12, 14) and "people of the land" (2:4). Some scholars maintain that the term "remnant" refers only to those who returned from exile in Babylon. However there is no indication it has that meaning here. While the term is used in Isaiah in the context of a return to the land, in Jeremiah and Ezekiel it is usually used of those who were left behind in the land after the Babylonian deportations.[34] As Hag 2:3 makes clear, the term refers rather to people who survived the Babylonian invasions and conquest.

The time of Babylonian domination lies in the past in Haggai. The only connection to an exile there comes from the book's references to

---

32. Williamson, "Comments," 36.

33. So, Japhet, *From the Rivers of Babylon*, 105.

34. On this, see Bedford, *Temple Restoration*, 55, 169; Japhet, *From the Rivers of Babylon*, 104, 432–36.

Zerubbabel and Joshua. According to Ezra 2:1, Zerubbabel was one of the exiles who returned to Yehud. A grandson of Jehoiachin, according to 1 Chr 3:19, he has a Babylonian name, *zer-babili*, which means "shoot of Babylon."[35] Joshua was the son of Jehozadak, and the grandson of Seraiah, both of whom were taken to Babylon (1 Chr 6:14, 15; 2 Kgs 25:18).[36]

The book has more to say about restoration than exile. The destruction of the temple meant Yhwh had either been defeated by some other deity or had abandoned his people. Their difficulties were compounded by dire economic times, which Haggai attributed to the delay in rebuilding the temple (1:5–6).[37] Rebuilding would prepare the way for Yhwh to return, be present with his people, and exercise his power for their welfare.[38] It is not clear how Haggai determined that the time had come to rebuild, but he had pointed to the economic situation as evidence of Yhwh's disfavor, and that the community should take action.

The book has a restorationist agenda, and it advances it in several different ways. The ancestry of the community's leaders—Zerubbabel and Joshua—is traced back to pre-587 Judah. They embody continuity with the past. The ruler-priest-prophet triad—Zerubbabel, Joshua, and Haggai—takes us back to pre-587 Judah with its Davidic king, temple priesthood, and prophets who confronted them. Unlike pre-587 Judah, where prophets attacked both ruler and priest, who were often aligned with each other, Haggai's situation is one in which prophet, priest, and ruler work together.[39]

The book also portrays a utopian future, brought about by the dramatic intervention of Yhwh, who "will shake the heavens, and the earth and the sea and the dry land" (2:6; also 2:21). One outcome is that Zerubbabel will be established as a future Davidic ruler:

> On that day, says the LORD of hosts, I will take you, O Zerubbabel my servant, son of Shealtiel, says the LORD, and make you like a signet ring; for I have chosen you, says the LORD of hosts.[40] (2:23)

---

35. Gerstenberger, *Israel in the Persian Period*, 100 The genealogical information in 1 Chr 3:19 is not straightforward, and is treated by Japhet, *From the Rivers of Babylon*, 57–58.

36. Japhet, *From the Rivers of Babylon*, 67–68.

37. The extent of the economic distress is difficult to judge, because he refers to people living in "paneled houses" (v. 4), implying that they were wealthy. Perhaps some were not affected by the economic troubles because of their wealth.

38. Bedford, *Temple Restoration*, 70–73.

39. Talmon, "'Exile' and 'Restoration,'" 134.

40. The expression "to make you like a signet ring" alludes back to the denunciation

The prophecy takes us beyond the horizon of history to a new idealised world order.⁴¹ Another outcome of Yhwh's shaking of the heavens and the earth is the elevation of the Jerusalem temple to a place of pre-eminence. Drawing on the language and imagery of the pre-exilic Zion theology, Haggai declares that the glory of the rebuilt temple will be greater than that of its Solomonic predecessor, and Yhwh will make Jerusalem a place of peace again.

So, the book is not interested in exile. It has a restorationist agenda, which focuses on the rebuilding of the temple. At the same time, it looks beyond that to a utopian vision of a future founded on a rebuilt temple more glorious than the original, and on the emergence a Davidic ruler. However the book recognizes the political reality of the time, as its superscription shows. The word from Yhwh comes to Haggai "in the second year of King Darius" to "Zerubbabel ... the governor of Judah" (1:1). Here Zerubbabel is called a "governor," a term used of local rulers in the Persian Empire.⁴² Regnal citations do not simply establish historical settings, but they also identify who has power at a particular time and place. Haggai 1:1 makes clear that "*the* king is not a Davidide but is rather a foreigner."⁴³

Zechariah 1–8

We will now look at how the ideas of exile and restoration are understood in Zech 1–8. Unlike the book of Haggai, Zech 1–8 is interested in the idea of the exile to Babylon, but situates it in a broader context of diaspora, the scattering of people from Judah into places other than (but including)

---

of Jehoiachin in Jer 22:24–28. In 22:24 Yhwh declares that if Jehoiachin (referred to here as Coniah) "were like the signet ring on my right hand ... I would tear you off and give you into the hands of those who seek your life." The reference is to the coming siege of Jerusalem by Nebuchadnezzar and the subsequent capture of Jehoiachin.

The idea that Zerubbabel would rule as a Davidic king is proposed by, e.g., Japhet, *From the Rivers of Babylon*, 63–64; Petersen, *Haggai & Zechariah 1–8*, 104–5; Talmon, "'Exile' and 'Restoration,'" 135 n.61.

A different view is that he will be a "vice-regent" of Yhwh, who is the real king of Yehud (so, Meyers and Meyers, *Zechariah 1–8*, 70). See also Rose, "Messianic Expectations," 169–73.

41. Japhet, *From the Rivers of Babylon*, 317.

42. In the NRSV, "governor" is the usual translation of the Hebrew פחה. See, e.g., Ezra 8:36; Neh 2:7, 9.

43. Petersen, *Haggai & Zechariah 1–8*, 282.

Babylon. Like Haggai, the vision of restoration in Zech 1–8 relates to the present created order, as well as to a utopian future.

Like the book of Haggai, Zech 1–8 gives insights into the community of Yehud in the early Persian period. The chapters refer to events from the years 520 (1:1, 7) and 518 (7:1), and reached their final form either in the late sixth or early fifth century BCE.[44] Zechariah 1–8 portrays the present as a moment of crisis for the community in Yehud. The problem is that while "the whole earth remains at peace" (1:11), Yhwh's mercy has not extended to Yehud:

> O Lord of hosts, how long will you withhold mercy
> from Jerusalem and the cities of Judah,
> with which you have been angry these seventy years? (1:12)

The origin of the present crisis lies in the past with the ancestors and their refusal to listen to the prophets and Yhwh: "They did not hear or heed me, says the Lord" (1:4). The same theme of the ancestors' rejection of the prophetic message also occurs in 7:8–14. As a consequence, the ancestors were scattered, as 1:18–31 and 7:14 make clear.

Zechariah 1–8 situates exile in the context of the scattering of the people. In 1:18–21 (2:1–3 MT) the prophet has a vision of four horns. While the exact significance of the vision is debated, these four horns are responsible for scattering "Judah, Israel, and Jerusalem" (v. 19, 21). The references to both Judah and Israel and the use of the verb to "scatter" broaden the meaning of exile. It now includes not only those deported from Judah by the Babylonians but also those deported from the northern kingdom by the Assyrians in 721.[45] Then 8:7 refers to people who have gone to unnamed places in the east and the west, and who will be gathered by Yhwh and brought to Yehud. So, in responding to the community's distress in the year 520 in Yehud, the book does not differentiate between those exiled by the Babylonians and those in diaspora, either in the early Persian period or the Assyrian.[46] The reference to Yhwh and his anger with the nations, and not just Babylon, also suggests that the book is concerned not only with exiles from Babylon but also with those who are scattered and living in various different countries. Yhwh will gather them, as well.

---

44. For a range of dates, see Kessler, "Diaspora and Homeland," 138, esp. n.1.

45. Kessler, "Diaspora and Homeland," 144–45. Similarly, Boda, "Scat! Exilic Motifs in the Book of Zechariah," 164.

46. "The text would thus appear to recognize a past, widespread dispersion and one more focused on Babylon" (Kessler, "Diaspora and Homeland," 146).

The references to Babylon in Zech 1–8 show it to be an ambiguous figure. In 2:7 there is the command: "Escape to Zion, you that live with daughter Babylon." Then 6:10 refers specifically to three men who have returned from exile in Babylon: Heldai, Tobijah, and Jedaiah. They have brought silver and gold with them for the rebuilding of the temple. Their presence points to a connection between the community in Babylon and that in Yehud, so that the former can be seen as an extension of the latter.[47] It is a place of exile, but ironically, also the source of financial support for the temple rebuilding. In 5:5–31, Babylon is a place of wickedness, in the form of idolatry. These verses are about a vision of a flying basket, which contains the figure of a woman identified as "wickedness" (v. 8), a term that equates with idolatry.[48] It is then carried by two stork-like figures to Shinar. According to Gen 10:10, Babylon is in the land of Shinar, which then figures in the well-known story of the tower of Babel (11:1–3). The vision then suggests a two-way transaction: exiles come from Babylon, idolatry is sent back to where it originated (i.e., Shinar) and Yehud is thus purified.[49]

The first element for consideration in Zechariah's restoration agenda is the return of Yhwh (1:10–12) and the consequent repopulation of Jerusalem. Another element in the restoration is the purification of the land, which was required because the destruction of the temple by the Babylonians would have polluted it. Zechariah 3 narrates the purification of the high priest Joshua. He is portrayed as having filthy clothes, which symbolize his guilt and that of the land. The vision of the flying basket is also about the purification of the land. The meaning of the basket flying to Shinar is that the guilt incurred by the destruction of the temple has now been removed. The land is now ready for the rebuilding of the temple.

The texts about the rebuilding have two dimensions. One is historical, the other utopian. The historical element is found in 4:9, according to which Zerubbabel laid the foundation stone for the rebuilt temple, and would bring the project to completion. Besides the temple, Jerusalem is also to be rebuilt and repopulated, events that are described in utopian terms:

---

47. So, Kessler, "Diaspora and Homeland," 150. In time the relationship becomes one of financial dependence of the poorer community in Yehud with the wealthier one in Babylon (Knoppers, "Construction," esp. 20–21).

48. Boda, *Zechariah*, 355; Conrad, *Zechariah*, 166–67.

49. So, Petersen, *Haggai & Zechariah 1–8*, 261. An allusion to the Babylon of the sixth century BCE is also proposed by Boda, "Terrifying the Horns," 28. For an opposite opinion, see Körting, "Sach 5,5–11."

> Jerusalem shall be inhabited like villages without walls,
> because of the multitude of people and animals in it.
> For I will be a wall of fire all around it, says the LORD,
> and I will be the glory within it. (2:4–5)

There is also an echo of the old Zion theology in Yhwh's promise to "again choose Jerusalem" (1:17; 2:12), and his promise to punish the nations for what they have done to "the apple of my eye" (2:8).[50]

The idyllic character of the future is also expressed in 8:4–3, according to which its inhabitants will live long lives while young children play around them. The city will become a blessing to such an extent that "many peoples and strong nations" will come up to it (8:13, 20–32). Zechariah 1–8 then concludes on a similar note:

> Thus says the LORD of hosts:
> In those days ten men from nations of every language
> shall take hold of a Jew, grasping his garment
> and saying, "Let us go with you,
> for we have heard that God is with you." (8:23)

Besides presenting a vision of the future, the book also shows how that future might come about. The community is called to learn the lessons of the past. It was the ancestors' sin that caused the present state of distress (1:4–6; 7:9–14; 8:14). So, the promised future depends on the fidelity of the existing community (1:3; 8:16–17).[51] At present it is only a small group, a "remnant," but it is called on to believe that what is promised can be realized (8:6).

EXILE AND RESTORATION IN EZRA AND NEHEMIAH

The book of Ezra in particular has its own very distinctive understanding of the exile (and the exiles), which is very different from that in Nehemiah, Haggai, and Zech 1–8. In Ezra, being an exile or being connected to the community of exiles from Babylon makes one an authentic Israelite. Ezra radically transforms the significance of the calamity of 587. The idea that the exile was a sign of Yhwh's disfavor is replaced by the understanding that to be an exile was an indicator of belonging to an exclusive community called Israel. The "returning exiles," as they are frequently called in the book, and

---

50. Bedford, *Temple Restoration*, 255–56; Conrad, *Zechariah*, 69.
51. Kessler, "Diaspora and Homeland," 148–49.

they alone, constitute the true Israel. Ezra constructs a version of events that occurred in the aftermath of Persia's conquest of Babylon in the sixth century, and uses it to advance the claims of a section of Judahite society two centuries later.[52] In what follows we will outline the book's version of events, and then show how they are fashioned to advance a theological agenda.

The Narrative of Ezra

The book of Ezra begins by taking up where the Chronicler's history of Israel leaves off. According to 2 Chr 36:17–21, the Babylonian conquest of Judah in 587 BCE and the subsequent deportations of its population left the land empty of inhabitants for a period of seventy years, as predicted by the prophet Jeremiah (Jer 25:11; 29:10).[53] The seventy-year period came to an end when the Persian emperor Cyrus appeared on the scene and issued a decree allowing the return of people to Jerusalem (2 Chr 36:23). Ezra 1:1 resumes 2 Chr 36:22, and then develops a fuller version of the decree (Ezra 1:2–3) than that found in 2 Chr 36:23. The decree allowed the survivors of the Babylonian exiles to go up to Jerusalem and rebuild its temple (Ezra 1:3–5). As they left, Cyrus gave them the precious vessels and implements that Nebuchadnezzar had taken from the Jerusalem temple and brought to Babylon (1:7–11).[54]

Ezra 2 gives a list of the names of approximately 50,000 people who returned and settled in the towns of Yehud. Some sacred rituals, such as burnt offerings and the celebration of Sukkoth (Tabernacles) were resumed, and the foundation stone for a rebuild temple was laid (Ezra 3). However the rebuilding ran into problems. The returned exiles were approached by a group who are identified as "the adversaries of Judah and Benjamin" (4:1). They offered their support to help rebuild the temple, but were rebuffed by the exiles. As a result, there was concerted opposition to the rebuilding, and an appeal was successfully made to the Persian king to stop the work. The conflict was resolved when the decree of Cyrus allowing the rebuilding was recovered from the royal archives, and the Persian authorities allowed the work to be completed (Ezra 5–3). The dedication of the temple was celebrated with great joy (6:16–18), and was then followed by the feast of

---

52. For further on the book of Ezra and its fifth-century agenda, see e.g., Bedford, *Temple Restoration*, 85–100.

53. On the empty land as a theological construct, see earlier pages 14–16.

54 The plundering of the temple is described in 2 Kgs 24:13–17; Jer 52:17–23.

Passover, and the seven days of unleavened bread, also occasions of great happiness (6:19–32).

The narrative next turns to the figure of Ezra, and describes his journey from Babylon and arrival in Jerusalem (Ezra 7–3). An official of the Persian administration, but also a descendant of Aaron and a scribe "skilled in the law of Moses" (7:6), he came from Babylon accompanied by 5,000 returning exiles (Ezra 8:1–34). Soon after his arrival in Jerusalem he was confronted with the problem of intermarriage—men who had returned from exile had married women from the neighboring peoples (9:1–3). Their action was considered as "faithlessness" (9:4), so Ezra prayed on their behalf, asking Yhwh not to punish them for their sin. After a night of fasting and prayer, he called an assembly of the people and directed the men to separate themselves from their foreign wives (chapter 10). A list of names of the men guilty of intermarriage is given in chapter 10. The book concludes: "All these had married foreign women, and they sent them away with their children" (10:44). In this way the integrity of "the holy seed" (9:2) was preserved.

The storyline in Ezra suggests that there was a return en masse by exiles soon after Cyrus had conquered Babylon. They rebuilt the temple, resumed the celebration of feasts such as Passover and Sukkoth, publicly proclaimed the Mosaic law, and separated themselves from the surrounding peoples as the Deuteronomic law commanded. The impression given by Ezra is that the returning exiles had restored the society that was pre-587 Judah, and that this happened relatively soon after Cyrus' conquest in 539.

The Agenda of the Book of Ezra

As noted above, the agenda of the book of Ezra reflects a dispute from the later Persian period about community and identity—who belonged to the community of Israel, and who did not? The book advanced the cause of one group, who are referred to as "the exiles." A connection with them defined who belonged to the community of Israel. The claims of the Ezra group were exclusive. Anyone who did not align themselves with "the exiles" did not belong. The claims were advanced by developing a narrative about a return to Judah of exiles from Babylon soon after 539. The narrative calls them "the sons of the exile," usually translated as "the returned exiles."[55]

---

55. Hebrew: בני הגולה—"the sons of the exiles." See the various translations such as, the NRSV, RSV, JPS Tanak.

THE EARLY PERSIAN PERIOD

By rebuilding the temple, reinstituting worship there, celebrating the traditional feasts, and separating themselves from the surrounding peoples, they showed that they were the inheritors of the sacred traditions of the past, and therefore they alone were the true Israel.

Their exclusive sense of identity is shown in the rebuilding of the temple, and by their claim that they alone were given this task. In 4:2 they were approached by a group of people, who called themselves fellow-travellers, worshipping the same God as the returned exiles, and offering to help in the work of rebuilding (v. 2). The narrative, however, calls them "the adversaries of Judah and Jerusalem" (4:1).[56] The returned exiles will have nothing to do with their offer, rejecting it by engaging in an inventive exegesis of the decree of Cyrus: "We alone will build to the LORD, the God of Israel, as King Cyrus of Persia has commanded us" (4:3). A comparison of 4:3 with the text of the decree in 1:2-3 shows two small but significant differences. Firstly, in 1:2-3 there is no reference to a command of Cyrus to rebuild the temple. Rather the decree is by way of a permission or an offer: If any one among you belongs to his people . . . let him go up (1:3).[57] Secondly, according to 4:3, it is only the exiles who are to do the rebuilding: "*We alone* will build."[58] However, according to the decree of Cyrus, the offer to rebuild is open to "any of those who are of his [the God of Israel's] people" (1:3).

In 6:19-32, which narrates the celebration of the Passover, the concept of the true Israel is expanded. The Passover was eaten by "the people of Israel who had returned from exile" and by those "who had joined them and separated themselves from the pollutions of the nations of the land" (v. 21). However, as 6:19 indicates, the returned exiles still remained as the core of the true Israel, and separation from "the peoples of the land" was required by those who join them. The celebration of Passover points is another indicator of the book's restoration agenda. By celebrating the great story of the deliverance from Egypt, another point of continuity is established between the Persian period community in Yehud and the pre-587 Judah.

The "exiles" also appeal to the exclusivism found in the book of Deuteronomy. Ezra 9-10 deals with the crisis of intermarriage, when their men had married foreign women. They solved the crisis by sending away the

---

56. The identity of this group is not clear. For a brief discussion of scholarship on this point, see Williamson, *Ezra, Nehemiah*, 49-50.

57. The translation here is that of Blenkinsopp, *Ezra-Nehemiah*, 74. For the relevant grammatical material on this point, see Joüon, *Grammar of Biblical Hebrew*, 376-77.

58 I use italics here to reflect the emphasis conveyed by the Hebrew word order.

foreign wives and their children. The solution was validated by an appeal to the past. Seeing themselves in continuity with the first generations who entered the land, the leaders of the Ezra group applied the Deuteronomic law on intermarriage to their situation. Deuteronomy 7:1–3 prohibited marriage between Israelites and the surrounding peoples, "seven nations mightier and more numerous than you" (v. 1). Ezra 9:1 drew on this list and also on Deut 23:1–3 to produce a list of nations whose behavior is said to have polluted or defiled the land, and so threatened Israel's possession of it.[59] The solution was the expulsion of the women and children so that the purity of the "holy seed" (Ezra 9:2) might be preserved. In Ezra 9–10 the past was used again to validate their exclusive claim to be the true Israel.[60]

The representation of Ezra himself, a theological construct, also involved creating a link to the past. In 7:1–3 there is the genealogy of Ezra, which traces his origins back to Aaron. According to v. 6 he is also "a scribe skilled in the law of Moses."[61] As priest and scribe he thus embodies what became the twin pillars of Second Temple Judaism: the temple and the law. Ezra's restorationist agenda was completed by events involving him, but which are narrated in the book of Nehemiah: namely, the rebuilding of the walls of Jerusalem, the repopulating of the city (Neh 2–4; 6–7), and Ezra's proclamation of the law to the assembled people (chap. 8).

Establishing identity by separation is also a central idea in Ezra. It continues the same dynamic as happened in the community in Babylon. There, rituals like circumcision, sabbath rest, and dietary restrictions functioned as identity markers. Now, in their life back in Yehud, the identity of the community is expressed by its practice of separating itself from the

---

59 The marriage crisis came about because "the people of Israel" (9:1) had married women who are variously described as belonging to "the peoples of the lands" (9:1–2) and "the peoples of the land" (10:2). The foreign wives are said to belong to Israel's ancient enemies—"the Canaanites, the Hittites, the Perizzites, the Jebusites, the Ammonites, the Moabites, the Egyptians, and the Edomites" (9:1). Prohibitions against including Ammonites and Moabites are found in Deut 23:3, but Deut 7:1–3 does not mention the Ammonites, the Moabites, or the Egyptians. Although Moabites and Ammonites cannot ever become part of the people of Israel (Deut 23:3), the prohibition does not extend to Egyptians (23:7).

60. The literature on Ezra 9–10 is extensive. For further, see e.g., Douglas, "Responding to Ezra"; Janzen, *Witch-Hunts, Purity and Social Boundaries*; Olyan, "Purity Ideology"; Smith, "The Politics of Ezra"; Washington, "The Strange Woman (אשה זרה/נכריה) of Proverbs 1—9 and Post-Exilic Judaean Society."

61. In Ezra 7 his role as a teacher of the Torah is mentioned a number of times: vv. 6, 10, 11, 12, 14, 21, 25 (the last five in the text of the letter of Artaxerxes).

surrounding peoples. Deuteronomic exclusivism provides the theological justification. Seeing themselves in continuity with the first generations who entered the land, the leaders of the Ezra group apply the Deuteronomic law on intermarriage to their situation.

Exile and Restoration in Ezra

The book of Ezra gives clear answers to the questions "did the exile end, and when?" and "was there a restoration?" Ezra 1:1 took off from where 2 Chr 36:22 left off. The exile ended with the rise of Cyrus and his defeat of the Babylonians. As a result, there was a return to the land of Judah by exiles from Babylon and a restoration of key institutions of pre-587 Judah.

In effect, the book of Ezra radically reinterprets the idea of exile. In texts such as Jeremiah, exile is linked with punishment. Invasion by an overpowering enemy and the taking of exiles are understood as divine punishment for Judah's evil behavior. In Ezra this link between exile and punishment is broken, and replaced with something more radical and positive: to be an exile, or to have some connection with the community of exiles, is a sign of a true Israelite. The book is not interested in exile as such, and makes no reference to people in the diaspora. As Japhet writes: "The topic of the book is the reconstruction of Israel in its land, and exile is only the place from which the Israelites are to come—as Moses and the people of Israel had done many generations before them."[62]

Similarly, the book uses the idea of restoration to validate its claims. It portrays the returning exiles as the authentic inheritors of the traditions of pre-587 Judah. It is the returning exiles who rebuild the temple, celebrate Passover, separate themselves from the "peoples of the land" who surround them, and liken themselves to the people who under the leadership of Joshua took possession of the promised land. At the head of this community is the figure of Ezra, who is portrayed both as teacher of Torah and a descendant of Aaron. In this way he embodies the two foundational pillars of Second Temple Judaism, the law and the cult. In Ezra, the restoration of past institutions is not an end in itself, but a means of justifying a claim to authentic belonging. Unlike in Haggai and Zech 1–8, the representation of restoration in Ezra is not idyllic, but is presented as something already realized. However, the restoration described in the book is a compromise. Ezra, supposedly the new Moses and the new Aaron, is actually an official

---

62. Japhet, *From the Rivers of Babylon*, 116.

of the Persian overlords. Not only his journey to Judah (Ezra 7) but indeed his overall program of restoration is completely dependent on the good graces of the Persian emperor.

The Book of Nehemiah

The unusual ending of Ezra—its account of the sending away the foreign wives and their children—has led some scholars to propose that it and Nehemiah were originally one book. However, the opening verses of Nehemiah do not provide any sense of a connection with Ezra 10, and there are important differences between the two that for some scholars have indicated the different authorship of the two books.[63] In Nehemiah exile does not figure as much as in Ezra, and the restoration agenda of the two also differs.

The Narrative of Nehemiah

Nehemiah 1:1 situates Nehemiah in Susa, one of the capital cities of the Persian Empire. The reference to "the twentieth year" in v. 1 has caused scholarly debate, and is commonly accepted as the year 445.[64] The book of Nehemiah focusses on his work of rebuilding the walls of Jerusalem, and in arranging for the repopulation both of the city and the countryside (Neh 2–4, 6–7) besides dealing with the problem of food shortages (Neh 5). Like Ezra, he had to overcome opposition from some of the neighboring peoples (Neh 4:1–23; 6:1–19). After the completion of the city walls, and the resettling of the returning exiles, the whole community gathered in Jerusalem to hear Ezra read from "the book of the law of Moses" (8:1). This marks the highpoint of the restoration program. There is a sense of completion because the Torah is reinstated, and another feature of pre-587 Judah was been restored. In response the people are moved to weep for joy (8:9), and celebrate with a feast of food and wine (v. 12). As the leaders studied the book of the law, they discovered the obligation to celebrate the feast of Tabernacles. They then ordered the celebration of the feast, which lasted for eight days, and on each day Ezra read from the book of the law (8:14–18).

---

63. See recently Amzallag, "The Authorship of Ezra and Nehemiah."
64. A detailed examination of the chronological problems in the books of Ezra and Nehemiah is given by Japhet, *From the Rivers of Babylon*, 254–60.

Then in Neh 9 there is a sudden shift in mood from one of celebration to one of penitence. Like Ezra 9, the issue was the relationship between the community and foreigners, but what precisely the problem was is not clear. In Neh 9:2 "the seed of Israel" publicly confess their sins, and Ezra responds with a long prayer asking Yhwh's forgiveness (9:6–37). The people enter into a covenant with Yhwh, and promise to "walk in God's law, which was given by his servant Moses" (10:3). The Nehemiah narrative concludes with the account of the repopulating of Jerusalem, and the enforcing of the prohibition to trade on the sabbath (Neh 11–13). Nehemiah's program meant that the once-great city of pre-587 Judah has now regained some of its importance and prestige.

The Agenda of Nehemiah

The issue that the book of Nehemiah addresses is the survival of the community, which it ensures by the rebuilding of the walls of Jerusalem and the repopulation of the city. It also has a clear political message: all this is guaranteed only through the acceptance of Persian hegemony. Where the focus of Ezra was on the restoration of the pre-587 religious institutions, that of Nehemiah is on the rehabilitation of the city of Jerusalem. Like Ezra, Nehemiah is a representative of the Persian emperor. He is dependent on the emperor's benevolence, and speaks against any suggestion that Yehud can exist as a nation independent of Persian control.

However, the book of Nehemiah presents a picture of Judah quite different to that portrayed in Ezra. Nehemiah presumes the existence of the temple in Jerusalem and a settled community in Yehud, but a city in disrepair with its walls and gates either destroyed or broken (Neh 1:3). Although the time of Babylonian occupation and the exile are over, Jerusalem still suffers from the shame associated with these events. Its inhabitants are "in great trouble and shame" (1:3; see also 2:17; 3:36; 5;9). The term "shame" is commonly used to describe the fate of Judah or its inhabitants at the hands of the Babylonian conqueror (e.g., Lam 5:1; Ezek 5:14, 15).[65] The continuing shame of Jerusalem in the time of Nehemiah indicates that aspects of the exile still are in play.

Nehemiah is grieved about the state of the city, and asks the Persian emperor if he can go to Jerusalem and rebuild it. His request is framed in personal terms: he asks to go to "the city of the tombs of my ancestors"

65. Hebrew: הרפה.

(2:5).⁶⁶ However, there is also a political dimension to his request. One effect of rebuilding the city walls was the strengthening of Persian control. Like any fortified city in the empire, Jerusalem would have had its garrison of soldiers whose main tasks were to control the inhabitants and protect the surrounding countryside.⁶⁷

The issue of submission to Persian control lies behind part of the prayer in Neh 10. The prayer consists of a long review of Israel's history (vv. 6–31) and a plea for Yhwh to free the community from its present troubles (vv. 32–37). The prayer attributes the present distress to the infidelity of the people from the time of the Assyrian Empire down to the present (v. 32). It summarizes the pain of the present distress:

> Here we are, slaves to this day—slaves in the land you gave our ancestors to enjoy its fruits and its good gifts.
> Its rich yield goes to the kings whom you have set over us because of our sins; they have power also over our bodies and over our livestock at their pleasure, and we are in great distress. (10:36–37)

As has been often noted, the anti-Persian sentiments in these verses stand in clear contrast to the otherwise positive representation of the Persians in the rest of the book.⁶⁸ Two interpretations of vv. 36–37 have been put forward. One is that, when these verses are read in the context of the covenant ceremony, they become "to some degree, an implied declaration of independence from their current political overlords."⁶⁹ However, when situated in the larger context of the book and its portrait of Nehemiah as a Persian official, it is hard to see them as a declaration of independence. Rather, as Janzen has suggested, they stand as a rebuttal of those who advocate the future independent of the Persians.⁷⁰ The similar confession in Ezra 9 also refers to the people's present distress and their condition as one of slaves, but interprets it much more positively: "For we are slaves; yet our God has not forsaken us in our slavery, but has extended to us his steadfast love before the kings of Persia" (9:9).

In Nehemiah the return of exiles from Babylon lies in the past. The only reference to exile or returning exiles is found only in Neh 7:6, which introduces the list of those who returned from Babylon but were by now

---

66. On Nehemiah's request, see Blenkinsopp, *Ezra-Nehemiah*, 214.
67. Fried, *The Priest and the Great King*, 194–96.
68. Janzen, "Yahwistic Appropriation," 841 n.3.
69. Duggan, *Covenant Renewal*, 232. See also Laird, *Negotiating Power*, 282.
70. Janzen, "Yahwistic Appropriation," 854–56.

well settled in their own towns. However, the shadow of the exile hangs over Jerusalem (1:3; 2:17). Still in ruins and without walls and a city gate, its condition is one of shame, a term that is often used to describe the situation of Judah, its land, and inhabitants after the Babylonian conquest and destruction of 587.[71] Although like Ezra, Nehemiah encountered resistance from elements of the local population, the book does not portray the community as so highly polarized. It describes opposition to Nehemiah's plans as coming from local officials in Yehud, such as Sanballat and Tobiah.[72] It reflects the political situation of the time, and the common conflicts that happened between Persian governors and local leaders.[73] There is no suggestion of a conflict between "returning exiles" and "the peoples of the land." The population of Yehud is simply referred to as "Jews."[74] The term "escape," used to refer to the returning exiles in Ezra 9:8, 13–15, is found in Neh 1:2, where Nehemiah enquires about "the Judeans that survived, those who had escaped the captivity." However, in the latter it simply refers also to those who had survived the Babylonian conquest but had not been deported.[75]

The book of Nehemiah has a broader understanding of community than that in Ezra. Included in the list of community members are people from beyond Judah's borders, areas that were under Edomite control at the time of Nehemiah (Neh 11:25–36).[76] Like Ezra, he opposed and forbad marriage with foreign women (1:23–27), but did not send the wives and children away. The prohibition was binding only for the future. At the same time, the book of Nehemiah advocated separation of the community "from all foreigners" (9:2). While both books emphasize the need for separation, there is an important difference between them. For Ezra, the community consisted only of those who identified themselves with "the returning exiles." For Nehemiah, however, the community had a broader composition, and did not have the ethnic exclusivism found in Ezra.

---

71. See n.65 above.

72. Sanballat was probably a governor of Samaria, while the identity of Tobiah is not clear. For further, see Blenkinsopp, *Ezra-Nehemiah*, 216–19; Briant, *From Cyrus to Alexander*, 587.

73. For detailed treatment of Sanballat, Tobiah and their roles in the politics of the time, see Fried, *The Priest and the Great King*, 201–12.

74. Hebrew: יהודים. Amzallag, "The Authorship of Ezra and Nehemiah," 276–77.

75. Amzallag, "The Authorship of Ezra and Nehemiah," 274–75.

76. Amzallag, "The Authorship of Ezra and Nehemiah," 279–80; Blenkinsopp, *Ezra-Nehemiah*, 329.

Exile and Restoration in Nehemiah

The exile in Nehemiah lies in the past, and the book contains only a couple of references to it. One is a passing reference in the census list of chapter 7. The other is in reference to the shame felt by Jerusalem and its inhabitants because its walls and gates still lay in ruins over a hundred years after the demise of Babylon and the rise of Persia. Its focus is on restoration, and specifically on the rebuilding and repopulation of Jerusalem. Restoration will mean the removal of the shame brought about by the destruction of the city during the Babylonian conquest and exile. However, like Ezra, Nehemiah was an official of the Persian Empire, and whatever he achieved in Jerusalem was also dependent on the good graces of a foreign overlord.

SUMMARY

In this chapter we have looked at the understandings of exile and restoration in texts that portray the early years of Judah's existence under the Persians. In the book of Ezra exile is a central concept. The book shows that there was a significant change in how the exile in Babylon was understood. Rather than being an expression of Yhwh's punishment of Judah, it became a marker of authenticity: exiles and those associated with them were the true Israel that set about the restoration of pre-587 institutions in Judah. In Ezra the exile of Judeans has ended. The appearance of Cyrus brought to an end the seventy years of Babylonian domination predicted by the prophet Jeremiah.

However, while the book of Ezra is situated in the years soon after 539, the book is actually a later composition. It comes from fifth or fourth centuries BCE and its contents reflect the conflict in the community about belonging and identity: who belongs to Israel and who does not. For Ezra, only those who claim to be exiles and those who attach themselves to that group can claim membership of the community of Israel. Paradoxically, in earlier texts such as Haggai and Zech 1–8, written perhaps a hundred years before Ezra, exile does not have the same significance.

In these earlier texts it is at best a backdrop for the events that they narrate. In Nehemiah, whose focus is the rebuilding of the walls of Jerusalem, it also stands in the background as an event from the past.

Restoration, the counter-figure to exile, is also a theological construct in the texts examined in this chapter. In Haggai and Zech 1–8, there were two aspects to restoration. One aspect focussed on the rebuilding of the Jerusalem temple as an event that would happen within the horizon of human history. The other aspect focussed on a utopian vision of the future with a temple greater and more magnificent than Solomon's, and the appearance of a Davidic ruler.

Haggai, Zech 1–8, Ezra, and Nehemiah all portray some form of restoration, but it is not in any way a total restoration of the foundations of pre-587 Judah. While each of the texts focussed on one or several aspects of the pre-587 institutions, the reality of Judah's existence after the Babylonians was still one of servitude. Restoration of any of the pre-587 institutions was completely dependent on the good grace of the Persians. It can be no accident that the books that describe restoration as a present happening have as their putative authors Ezra and Nehemiah, two men who were appointees of the Persian overlords.

Chapter 6

THE UNENDED EXILE

THE FURTHER WE MOVE away from the neo-Babylonian period, the more important the idea of exile becomes. Haggai and Zech 1–8, texts that were composed not long after the demise of Babylon, show much less interest in the exile than does the book of Ezra, which was composed at least a hundred years later. By the time of the Maccabees, the figure of exile takes on further importance, as what follows in this chapter will show. The community of Israel, whether living in the land or outside it, is portrayed as *still in exile*, and *still waiting a return to the homeland*. Exile has now been reinterpreted, and has become a paradigm that the biblical writers in the late Second Temple period used to interpret the situation of their own times.

In this chapter we explore those situations that gave rise to the belief that the exile had not yet ended. The texts to be read here are from Isa 56–66, Jeremiah MT, the books of Daniel and Baruch.

ISAIAH 56–66

Isaiah 56–66 address a disillusioned community living in Yehud in the Persian period. Originating from a later time, chapters 56–66 take up some of the great themes of chapters 40–55. However, unlike the latter, chapters 56–66 reflect the disillusionment of the community. The marvelous utopian visions of chapters 40–55 had not materialized. Although the words "exile" and "exiles" do not occur in Isa 56–66, these chapters express the community's disillusionment in language frequently used in other texts to describe the devastation of Judah by the Babylonians in 587, and the deportation to Babylon of various groups of the population. The chapters thus portray the community as if they were still in exile, although they were now living in the Yehud of the Persian period.

Isaiah 61:1–3

We begin with 61:1–3, the "conceptual and structural center of chs. 60–62."[1] The earliest section of chapters 56–66 is chapters 60–62, and its kernel is 61:1–3.

> The spirit of the LORD GOD is upon me,
> because the LORD has anointed me;
> he has sent me to bring good news to the oppressed,
> to bind up the brokenhearted,
> to proclaim liberty to the captives, and release to the prisoners;
> to proclaim the year of the LORD's favor,
> and the day of vengeance of our God; to comfort all who mourn;
> to provide for those who mourn in Zion—
> to give them a garland instead of ashes,
> the oil of gladness instead of mourning,
> the mantle of praise instead of a faint spirit.
> They will be called oaks of righteousness,
> the planting of the LORD, to display his glory. (61:1–3)

The message is addressed to a community characterized by mourning, oppression, being broken-hearted, and as having a "faint spirit."

The speaker, as the herald of good news (61:1), has the same mission as the messenger addressed in 40:9: "herald of Zion," an image also found in 52:7: "How beautiful upon the mountains are the feet of the herald who announces peace."[2] The context of 52:7 is a text (52:1–7) that announces the reign of Yhwh's return to Zion (v. 8), the liberation and elevation of Jerusalem (vv. 1–3), and the call to leave Babylon (vv. 11–12). So, although a herald had been commissioned to announce good news to the community (chapters 40–55), there was a need for another commissioning, because the expected good news had not eventuated, and a disillusioned community was still waiting for the promised deliverance. There are three references to

---

1. Gregory, "The Postexilic Exile," 479. For further, see Blenkinsopp, *Isaiah 56–66*, 38–39.

2. Hebrew: לבשׂר (61:1); מבשׂרת (40:9); מבשׂר (52:7).

people mourning in 61:2, 3, an end of which is promised in 60:20—"Your days of mourning shall be ended." Similarly 61:2 says that the herald will bring "comfort to all who mourn," something previously proclaimed in 49:13; 51:2 (x2), 12, and 52:9, but especially at the very beginning of chapters 40–55: "Comfort, o comfort my people" (40:1). Again, the promise has not yet been realized.

The good news of 61:1–3 is addressed firstly to the "oppressed" and the "brokenhearted," people who are materially destitute.[3] 61:1 also promises "liberty to captives." The word "liberty" points us to Lev 25 and its description of the jubilee year, when all debts will be cancelled.[4] According to Lev 25:10, not only will captives be set free, but everyone will be able to return their own property and family. In the ancient Near East, a king granted liberty on special occasions, and one form of that was the repatriation of exiles.[5] So the reference in 61:1 may well be an allusion to the idea that the exile had not yet ended.

61:4 reinforces this idea by its use of language associated with exile. It refers to the rebuilding that those addressed in 61:1–3 will carry out:

> They shall build up the ancient ruins,
> they shall raise up the former devastations;
> they shall repair the ruined cities,
> the devastations of many generations. (61:4)

There is also a reference to "ruins" in 44:26, which proclaim a new future for Jerusalem: "'It shall be inhabited', and of the cities of Judah, 'They shall be rebuilt, and I will raise up their ruins.'" The references to ruins, desolation, and devastation take us back to earlier parts of the book of Isaiah, one of which is Isa 49:19. Its context, 49:14–21, opens with a complaint by Zion that Yhwh has abandoned her (v. 14), followed by an oracle refuting the claim (vv. 15–21). Yhwh's response is that, just as a mother cannot abandon her own child, so he cannot abandon his people. Not only will the bereaved and barren Zion have children, they will be so numerous that the land will be overcrowded (v. 19): "Surely your ruins and your desolate places and your devastated land—surely now you will be too crowded for your inhabitants . . . ."

---

3. Gregory, "The Postexilic Exile," 482.
4. Gregory, "The Postexilic Exile," 483.
5. Lynch, "Zion's Warrior and the Nations," 260.

A similar promise is in 54:1–3, according to which "the children of the desolate woman will be more than the children of her that is married" (v. 1), and they will "settle in the desolate towns" (v. 3). So, according to 61:4, the land is still devastated, and awaits rebuilding. It is still in the same condition as it was after the Babylonian invasion.

So Isa 61:1–3 portrays the community as *still awaiting* the comfort promised in 40:1, the removal of poverty, the rebuilding and repopulating of the land. All these events associated with the end of the exile have yet to be realized.

Other Texts in Isaiah 56–66

Besides the texts examined above, there are other expressions in Isa 56–66 of a community divided, disillusioned, and feeling abandoned—all conditions associated in chapters 40–55 with being in exile in Babylon. 56:1–3, the beginning of Third Isaiah, is about a divided community. The community's distress gives rise to doubts about Yhwh and his power, which are countered in chapter 59: "See, the LORD's hand is not too short to save, nor his ear to dull to hear." The arm is a symbol for power. The references to Yhwh's arm go back to the deliverance from Egypt, when he brought the people out "by mighty hand and outstretched arm" (Deut 4:34).[6] In chapters 40–55, Yhwh's deliverance of the exiles is presented as such a wondrous event that it will surpass even the exodus from Egypt. The promise is that the God of the exodus will again act on Israel's behalf, and nothing can stop this divine intervention (43:13). The exiles are exhorted: "Do not remember the former things, or consider the things of old. I am about to do a new thing" (Isa 43:18–19a). The reality, however, fell far short of that, and the community was still waiting for that new thing (65:17).

63:17—64:12 (MT 64:11) is a communal lament, which expresses the people's sense of abandonment.[7] Its lament is filled with graphic language about the community's sense of despair, as its concluding verses show. In the silence that accompanies a sense of Yhwh's absence, the people question what might he do: "After all this, will you restrain yourself, O LORD? Will you keep silent and punish us so severely?" (v. 12). Verse 10 contains the

---

6. Blenkinsopp, *Isaiah 56–66*, 187.

7. The lament is treated in detail by Bautch, *Developments in Genre*, 29–63, esp. 36–40. See also the briefer treatments: Blenkinsopp, *Isaiah 56–66*, 257–66; Childs, *Isaiah*, 522–26.

plea "Do not be exceedingly angry, O LORD," an expression that occurs in a more enigmatic form at the end of the book of Lamentations: "are you are angry with us beyond measure?"[8] The issue left unresolved at the end of Lamentations is answered here: Yes, Yhwh was angry beyond measure, and the present destruction is evidence of that. As Blenkinsopp has said, "in writings from the post-destruction period, there is no more poignant expression of abandonment and godforsakenness than that expressed in 64:8–12."[9] The enigmatic and unfinished conclusion to the book of Lamentations is quite understandable in the light of the events of 587: the destruction and the deportations that followed the Babylonian conquest. However, the conclusion to the lament in 64:12 reveals a similar level of distress, incomprehension, and a sense of abandonment, yet it was composed in circumstances that were meant to be different. Lamentations 5:22 is set against the backdrop of the destruction and deportations of 587, whereas Isa 64:12 is set in the Persian period when the exile was supposedly ended and the restoration had supposedly taken place.

The great promises found in Isa 40–55 that the exiles would return from Babylon in a new exodus, and that the land of Judah would flourish, were never realized. For the tradents who gave us Isa 56–66, life is still much the same as before the advent of Cyrus. Living in the land of Yehud, is like still being in exile.

THE BOOK OF JEREMIAH MT

In Jeremiah MT, which reached its final form in the Persian period at the earliest, we have a more explicit expression that although the Babylonians have come and gone, the exile has not yet ended.[10]

Scholars have long recognized that the book of Jeremiah has a long compositional history that extends beyond the Persian period and down to the Hellenistic.[11] The book has come down to us in two very different

---

8. Hebrew: אל־תקצף יהוה מאד (Isa 64:8); קצפת עלינו עד־מאד (Lam 5:22).

9. Blenkinsopp, *Isaiah 56–66*, 264–65. For the similarities between 64:12 and the book of Lamentations, see ibid., 265–66.

10. "The overarching perspective of the finished book of Jeremiah is that Babylon stands and the exile has not ended" (Shead, *A Mouth Full of Fire*, 216).

11. The period between 515 and 445 (between the completion of the Jerusalem temple and the era of Nehemiah and Ezra) is proposed by Goldman, *Prophétie*, 143–47. The third and fourth centuries is the period favored by Stipp, *Das Sondergut*, 142–43.

versions, a shorter Greek version (LXX) and a longer Hebrew one (MT), which is a later recension than the former.[12] The MT of Jeremiah has characteristics that are quite different to those of the Greek, and are especially relevant here. Two significant characteristics are its interest in Babylon, not found in the LXX, and its understanding that the exile has not yet ended. So, on the one hand, we have the later recension in which Babylon is a key figure, and yet did not reach its final form until long after Babylon's demise. On the other hand we have a recension whose origins are closer to the neo-Babylonian era, and yet it gives less prominence to Babylon. So, the further we move away from the neo-Babylonian era, the more significant the literary figure of Babylon becomes.[13]

Babylon in Jeremiah MT: From the Historical to the Mythic

Jeremiah MT gives us a complex and distinctive portrayal of Babylon. Besides the conventional negative representation of Babylon as the great enemy, found in Jer 50–51, and in texts such as such as Isa 13–14 and Ps 137, Jeremiah MT also provides a contrasting and positive portrayal, not found in the Greek recension of the book.[14] Jeremiah MT's distinctive portrayal is seen especially in its representation of Nebuchadnezzar, the Babylonian emperor and conqueror of Judah.

He is more than just an instrument of Yhwh's judgment against Judah. Where Assyria was called "the rod of my anger" (Isa 10:5), Nebuchadnezzar is much more. At one point in the book he appears as Yhwh's partner in the siege of Jerusalem. In Jer 21:5–6 Yhwh declares that he himself is waging war against Jerusalem. Then in the next verses we are told that the city and

---

Perhaps the most extreme view is that of Duhm, who believed the book did not reach its final form until the first century BCE (Duhm, *Das Buch Jeremia*, X).

12. The existence of the two versions has caused much debate about their origins and how they relate to each other. The usual presumption in textual criticism has been that Greek texts are translations of older Hebrew ones, and that shorter texts are older than longer ones. However, texts discovered at Qumran have made these presumptions obsolete. The two recensions of the book of Jeremiah are a case in point. Scholars are now proposing that our present Greek version of Jeremiah was translated from a Hebrew text that both differs from, and is older than our present Masoretic text. A good survey of relevant scholarship is given by Gesundheit, "LXX Jeremiah," 29–36.

13. The role of Babylon in the Jeremiah tradition is treated extensively in Hill, *Friend or Foe?*

14. In what follows I am dependent on Hill, *Friend or Foe?* Also see my Hill, "Your Exile."

its inhabitants will be given into the hands of Nebuchadnezzar, who "will not spare them or have compassion" (v. 7). In the corresponding place in Jeremiah LXX, it is *Yhwh* who "will not spare them" or "have compassion."[15] Perhaps the most striking aspect of Nebuchadnezzar's portrayal in Jeremiah MT is that Yhwh refers to him as "my servant" (25:9), something not found in the LXX. The designation is startling because the only other people described as "my servant" are Abraham (Gen 26:24), Moses (Num 12:7), David (2 Sam 7:5, 8), and Isaiah (20:3). Nebuchadnezzar's special status in the eyes of Yhwh is further developed in Jeremiah 27 MT. The background to Jer 27:5–6 is the creation account in Gen 2. Here he is more a mythical than historical figure, and portrayed as a new Adam.[16] Besides being given the lands he has conquered, Nebuchadnezzar is given "even the wild beasts to serve him" (27:6). What is promised to the first human in Gen 2:15 is affirmed also about Nebuchadnezzar.

Nebuchadnezzar's quasi-mythical representation is part of a larger strategy in Jeremiah MT, where the historical figure of sixth-century Babylon is developed into a figure who transcends both time and space, and represents a power that is opposed to Yhwh.[17] The transition can be clearly seen in Jer 25 MT, but it is not in the LXX equivalent. The Babylon described in 25:1–14 MT resembles the historical Babylon that invaded Judah in the sixth century BCE, but in vv. 15–39 it morphs into a figure who transcends the limitations of history. Verses 15–39 describe a judgment scene in which the nations surrounding Judah submit themselves to Yhwh. In vv. 15–36 various nations are named, and then in v. 29 the judgment is extended to all the nations of the earth:

> All the kings of the north, far and near, one after another,
> and all the kingdoms of the world that are on the face of the earth.
> And after them the king of Sheshach shall drink. (25:29 MT)

There are two points about v. 29 to note. The first is the use of a code name, Sheshach, for Babylon.[18] The code adds a note of mystery, hiding the identity of the figure it represents. The second point is the relationship

---

15. For more detail, see Hill, *Friend or Foe?* 78–80.
16. Hill, "Your Exile," 154–55.
17. For a full treatment, see Hill, *Friend or Foe?* 120–24.
18. The code in v. 29 is based on the Hebrew word for Babylon, not the English. The code is known as an *athbash*, "in which the letters of a name counted from the beginning of the alphabet are exchanged for letters counted from the end" (Thompson, *Jeremiah*, 518 n.13. See also Hill, *Friend or Foe?* 122 n.65).

between Sheshach and the other nations, both named and unnamed in vv. 15–26. According to v. 26, "all the nations on the face of the earth will drink," but Sheshach is not included in the list of them found in vv. 18–36. It stands apart from all the other nations, as the Hebrew structure and grammar of vv. 15–26 make clear.[19] Sheshach is a figure of mystery, founded on but transcending the historical Babylon.

The transformation both of Nebuchadnezzar, and hence Babylon, to a transhistorical figure forms one part of Jeremiah MT's representation of the exile as unended. Babylon is *still* dominant, Judah is *still* desolate, and there are *still* Judahite exiles.

Jeremiah MT and Its Exilic Frame

The other element that contributes to the idea of the unended exile is the very structure of Jeremiah MT.[20] The book begins and ends in exile. In its superscription, it describes the ministry of Jeremiah as extending from 627 down to 587. However, the superscription does not correspond to the chronology of the book, which relates evens that happened after 587. Also, according to 1:2–3, his ministry covered a forty-year period. If we keep in mind that forty can often have a symbolic meaning and take into account that the book narrates events that happened after 587, then we are left with the question: how can we interpret this historically inaccurate superscription? To answer this question we need to consider how the book ends.

Where the superscription takes us up to the year 587, the book's concluding chapter begins with the events of that same year. It describes the siege and fall of Jerusalem (52:1–31), and their aftermath, including the deportations of some of the population. The chapter concludes with vv. 31–34, which describe the imprisonment of Jehoiachin, the Judahite king, and his place in the court of the Babylonian emperor. 52:31–34 situates these events in the year 560 BCE. So the book's superscription and its conclusion both refer to the year 587. The significance of this observation is important:

---

19. The nations other than Sheshach are the grammatical subjects of the verb ואשקה (*hifil* form of the verb—"and I made them drink" [v. 17]). However, in v. 26b the syntax is different: ומלך ששך ישתה אחריהם ("*and the king of Sheschach* will drink after them"). The placement of מלך ששך together with the use of the *qal* form of the verb gives emphasis to the king of Sheshach.

20. For what follows here, see Hill, "Your Exile," 156–58. There is a fuller treatment in Hill, *Friend or Foe?* 210–17.

Where 1:1-3 moves from the time of Josiah through to the year 587, chap. 52 resumes the events of 587 and moves through to the year 560, when the community is still in exile. The book is thus contained in an "exilic envelope." It begins and ends in exile, an exile which still continues.[21]

Although the book did not reach its final form until at least the early Persian period, the book's perspective is one of continuing exile. While the Babylonians have gone, Babylon has not, and so the exile continues.

The book's juxtaposition of promises of judgment and salvation also reflect the book's portrayal of an exile as yet unended. The book of Jeremiah contains sudden switches from doom to salvation and vice versa. The vision of a return of the earth to the state of primal chaos (4:23-26) is then mitigated by v. 27b: "The whole land shall be a desolation; yet I will not make a full end." Similarly in the middle of material about death and expulsion from the land (chapters 16-17) there is an *ex abrupto* appearance of a promise of a new exodus (16:14-15). This happens also at the macro level in the book, where large blocks of salvation material are circumscribed by promises of judgment. Chapters 29-33 consist nearly exclusively of promises of restoration and return to the land. However, they are embedded in a section of the book (chapters 26-36) that concludes with a proclamation of that the divine judgment is inevitable (36:17-21). Near the end of the book in its Hebrew form, the oracles against the nations (chapters 46-51) are immediately followed by another narrative of Jerusalem's fall in 587. The book then begins and ends in exile.

Jeremiah MT and the Unended Exile

In summary, the idea of the exile as unended is produced by the following three mechanisms.[22] The first is the development in the construction of the figure of Babylon where it morphs from a figure within history to the transhistorical Sheshach. At the end of the book, Babylon remains unconquered. The second is the framing of the book. Its beginning point is the year 587,

---

21. Hill, *Friend or Foe?* 26.

22. My view about the exile as unended in the book of Jeremiah MT is based on the final form of the book. Disagreeing with my view that Jeremiah was no more than a contributor to the belief in an unended exile, Shead writes that "Jeremiah was the origin, not simply a contributor... to the postexilic belief in an unended exile" (Shead, *A Mouth Full of Fire*, 216 n.71).

and it concludes with a reference to events that took place around the year 550. The third is the juxtaposition of promises of judgement and salvation in the book. One undermines the other, so that a tension exists in the text. There will be a future deliverance, but it is not yet realized.

THE BOOK OF DANIEL

The book of Daniel provides us with the clearest example so far of how the exile functioned as a paradigm that the book's authors used to interpret the situation that faced the community of their time. The book in its final form addressed the crisis in Judea in the second century BCE. However, at its beginning it situates its hero, the young man Daniel, in the court of Babylon during the reign of Nebuchadnezzar after he had conquered Jerusalem. Daniel is an exile, brought to Babylon by its king, where he stays for the duration of the whole book. There is no suggestion in the book that either he or any group of exiles returned to the homeland. In this chapter we will examine how the events of 587 and the exile are used to interpret the crisis in Judea in the second century BCE. There are two texts that reflect the book's understanding of exile. These are chapters 1 and 9. Chapter 1 provides a chronological framework in which the narratives and visions in the book are situated. Chapter 9 contains the reference to the seventy years of devastation for Jerusalem (9:2). However, before that, there are some preliminary issues about the book's interpretation that we need to address.

Daniel 1: The Exilic Setting

The book contains several chronological markers that set the book in the period of the neo-Babylonian and Persian Empires. Daniel 1:1 refers to the siege of Jerusalem by Nebuchadnezzar. Chapters 2–4 are also set in his reign, while chapters 5 and 7–8 are set in the time of Belshazzar. Then chapters 6, 9, and 11 are in the time of Darius, and chapter 10 in that of Cyrus.

The opening verses establish the book's setting:[23]

> In the third year of the reign of Jehoiakim king of Judah, Nebuchadnezzar king of Babylon came to Jerusalem and besieged it.
> And the LORD gave Jehoiakim king of Judah into his hand, with some of the vessels of the house of God; and he brought them to

23. Koch, *Daniel*, 13.

the land of Shinar, to the house of his god, and placed the vessels in the treasury of his god.[24] (1:1–2)

The book's central theological issue is reflected in v. 2. The siege and destruction of Jerusalem by Nebuchadnezzar was brought about by Yhwh: *he* gave Jehoiakim into the hand of Nebuchadnezzar. Verse 2 points to the dilemma that these events posed. If Nebuchadnezzar was able to destroy the temple, take away its sacred vessels, and put them in the temple of his own gods, does that mean Yhwh was and is powerless? At the same time, v. 2 points to Yhwh's control over history. The Babylonian conquest did not happen because their deities were more powerful than Yhwh. Rather, *Yhwh* brought about the conquest, and can therefore also bring about an end to Judea's present suffering and distress.[25]

The question about the apparent impotence of Yhwh was one that the community had struggled with over the centuries, as one empire replaced another and became the overlords of Syria-Palestine from the sixth century BCE down to the time of the Maccabean uprising. Faced with the domination of the Seleucids and their profaning of the Jerusalem temple, the community's faith was again called into question. The book of Daniel was composed before the victory of the Maccabees, and so it does not provide any information about the resolution of the crisis caused by the Seleucids. According to v. 2, Jehoiakim and the temple vessels are brought "to the land of Shinar." The term "Shinar" is a relatively rare word in the OT, but occurs in important contexts. In Gen 11:1–3 it is the site of the tower of Babel, which came to symbolize human pride and wilfulness. A further negative note to it is found in Zech 5:11, where Shinar is the destination for the basket containing "Wickedness."[26] It is a place of evil. Bringing the temple vessels there adds to the existing sense of desecration caused by the plundering of the Jerusalem temple, and by the placing of the vessels in the temple of a Babylonian deity.[27]

Does the book have anything to say about the duration of the exile, and when it might end? Daniel 1:21 provides a hint about the answer to the question: "And Daniel continued there until the first year of King Cyrus." So his stay in the court covers the "exilic" period as understood by

---

24. The translation here is that of the RSV, which is closer to the MT than that of the NRSV.

25. Kirkpatrick, *Competing for Honor*, 47; Willis, *Dissonance*, 57–59.

26. See earlier on pages 75–76.

27. On Shinar, see Goldingay, *Daniel*, 15; Kirkpatrick, *Competing for Honor*, 40–41.

the book of Ezra (1:1), where the appearance of Cyrus indicates the end of Babylonian domination, and a return of both exiles and the temple vessels to Jerusalem. However, in Daniel there is no clear indication of an end of exile. The question is addressed in chapter 9, but the answer provided there gives no readily understood meaning.[28] The chronological information in 1:21 differs from that found later in the book. According to 10:1, Daniel is still at court in the third year of Cyrus, but as Collins remarks, "here, as throughout the Book of Daniel, the release of Jewish exiles in the first year of Cyrus is ignored."[29] In 10:1, and also as indicated in 6:1 and 9:1, the Babylonian Empire has been superseded by the Persian and there is no change in Daniel's situation. He is still an exile.

Daniel 9 and the "Desolations of Jerusalem"

Daniel 9 continues the theme, found in chapter 8, of the destruction and desecration of the Jerusalem temple.[30] Chapter 8 ends with Daniel's dismay over the vision he has just had, and his inability to understand it. The idea of understanding or perceiving concludes chapter 8 and appears then early in chapter 9:[31]

> In the first year of his [Darius'] reign, I, Daniel, perceived in the books the number of years that, according to the word of the LORD to the prophet Jeremiah, must be fulfilled for the devastation of Jerusalem, namely, seventy years. (9:2)

Here the issue is the exile and its duration. According to the chronology of the book, the first year of Darius is 538 or 539, the end of Babylonian domination.[32] The books referred to in v. 2 are some form of Jeremiah, where Daniel finds a reference to a seventy-year duration of Babylonian dominance and exile in Jer 25:11–12 and 29:10. Daniel is disturbed by the Jeremian prophecy because Babylonian domination has ended, and exile still continues. The expression translated in the NRSV as "the devastation of Jerusalem" occurs only in one other place in the OT, Isa 52:9: "Break forth together into singing, you ruins of Jerusalem; for the LORD

---

28. According to 10:1, Daniel is still in the court in the third year of Cyrus.
29. Collins, *Daniel*, 372.
30. Collins, *Daniel*, 359; Goldingay, *Daniel*, 238.
31. The Hebrew verb בין is variously translated as "to perceive" or "to understand."
32. So, Bergsma, "Daniel 9.1–27," 53; Seow, *Daniel*, 138–39.

has comforted his people, he has redeemed Jerusalem."[33] The context of Isa 52:9 is an exodus-like return of exiles from Babylon, which promises a future for "the devastation of Jerusalem." In Dan 9 then "the devastation of Jerusalem" refers to an existing situation, the destruction of the city and also the deportation of its inhabitants.

The seventy-year prophecy of Jeremiah (9:2) also refers to both the end of Babylonian occupation and the return of exiles. There are two seventy-year prophecies in the book of Jeremiah. One is in 25:11–12, which predict the length of Judah's subjugation to Babylon (v. 11) and the latter's destruction (v. 12). The other is in 29:10, which predicts that, "after Babylon's seventy years are completed," the exiles will be returned from there to Judah. However, the end of Babylonian dominance did not necessarily signal that good times were ahead for Judah and its exiles in Babylon. Like earlier generations after the demise of the neo-Babylonian Empire, Daniel's community was still under the domination of a foreign invader, and was asking "when will it end?" The prophecy of Jeremiah had not been fulfilled.

Daniel's next move is to pray (vv. 3–39), but before doing so, he puts on sackcloth and ashes (v. 3), a normal preparation for prayer. The sackcloth and ashes also lend a penitential character to the prayer, as vv. 5–11 clearly show. The purpose of the prayer is not for Daniel to understand the meaning of the Jeremian prophecy, as the NRSV's translation of v. 3 suggests: "I turned to the Lord God, to seek an answer by prayer and supplication." Rather, as the more literal translation of the RSV indicates, the aim of the prayer was to seek Yhwh and to ask for forgiveness: "I turned my face to the Lord God, seeking him by prayer and supplication" (9:2). As the prayer shows, Daniel knew why the prophecy had not been fulfilled, and so begins the prayer with an extended plea for forgiveness. The prayer does not contain reference to any specific wrongdoing. Based on Deuteronomistic theology, it does not accuse the people of being unfaithful to Yhwh, but confesses unspecified transgressions and failures.[34]

The prayer interprets diaspora as the punishment for the people's "treachery" (v. 7). Guilt belongs not just to Daniel's generation, but to the whole people: "our kings, our officials, and our ancestors" (v. 8; also v. 16),

---

33. The Hebrew word חרבות is variously translated as "ruins" or "devastation"

34. The prayer is similar to other penitential prayers from the Second Temple period: e.g., Ezra 9:16; Neh 1:5–11; Bar 1:15—3:8 (Collins, *Daniel*, 349–50). For a list of Deuteronomistic expressions in the prayer, see Collins, *Daniel*, 349–52; also Goldingay, *Daniel*, 234.

i.e., people from the period before 587.³⁵ After the confession of guilt, the prayer concludes with an appeal to Yhwh to "hear ... forgive ... listen and act" (v. 19).

A response follows in vv. 20-27, and comes quickly, even as Daniel is still praying.³⁶ Daniel is told that "at the beginning of your supplication a word went out" (v. 23). The message that Gabriel brings is not actually a response to Daniel's prayer, but is rather a revelation or reinterpretation of the Jeremian prophecy (v. 24):

> Seventy weeks are decreed for your people and your holy city: to finish the transgression, to put an end to sin, and to atone for iniquity, to bring in everlasting righteousness, to seal both vision and prophet, and to anoint a most holy place. (9:24)

"Seventy weeks" then really means seventy weeks of years—i.e., 490 years. The calculation is based on the jubilee legislation in Lev 25:8, where the expression "seven weeks" means forty-nine years. So seventy weeks means 490 years.³⁷ Verse 24 then explains what needs to happen before the exile can be considered as ended. It contains six verbal infinitives with Yhwh as their implied subject.³⁸ The transgression referred to in v. 24 is either the action of Antiochus IV in desecrating the temple, or the cooperation given him by Jews in doing so, or both.³⁹ The sealing of the vision and the prophet means that the prophetic message here is authentic, and the anointing "of a most holy place" refers to the rebuilding and dedication of the Jerusalem temple.⁴⁰

The future of Jerusalem is then revealed:

---

35. "It is a common human experience that one generation will pay for the wrongdoing of the previous generation; the exile, in particular, resulted from the actions of earlier generations, as well as those of the people actually alive in the sixth century B.C." (Goldingay, *Daniel*, 246).

36. Seow, *Daniel*, 145.

37. For further on the computation of 490 years, see e.g., Collins, *Daniel*, 352-53; Seow, *Daniel*, 148-49; Fishbane, *Biblical Interpretation in Ancient Israel*, 482-85; Goldingay, *Daniel*, 257-58; also Kratz, "Visions," 109-11.

38. The verbs in question are: to finish, put an end to, atone, bring, seal, anoint. See Collins, *Daniel*, 353; Ulrich, *The Antiochene Crisis*, 37.

39. Besides 9:24, the word "transgression" (פשע) in the book of Daniel occurs only in chapter 8 (vv. 12, 13, 25), where the context is the desecration of the temple by Antiochus Epiphanes. For opinions on this, see Collins, *Daniel*, 354; Ulrich, *The Antiochene Crisis*, 39.

40. On sealing as indicating authenticity, see Goldingay, *Daniel*, 259-60.

> Know therefore and understand: from the time that the word went out to restore and rebuild Jerusalem until the time of an anointed prince, there shall be seven weeks; and for sixty-two weeks it shall be built again with streets and moat, but in a troubled time. (v. 25)

While the precise meaning of some of the verse is unclear, there is no ambiguity about the fate of Jerusalem. The expression "to restore and rebuild" means both rebuilding the Jerusalem temple and the return of its exiled population."[41] There are different opinions about the meaning of "the word that went out." It may refer to back to v. 23 and what was revealed to Daniel, or it may refer to the edict of Cyrus allowing the rebuilding of the Jerusalem temple.[42] The identity of the "anointed prince" is also not clear, but it may possibly refer to the early Persian-period figure of the high priest Joshua or his Maccabean-era descendant, Onias III. The latter was removed from the office of priest after Antiochus IV invaded Judea in 175 BCE.[43]

A feature of Dan 9, as with other apocalyptic literature, is the representation of time in terms of fixed periods. The use of jubilees in this way is found in other late Second Temple literature. In Dan 9 it allows the author to put forward a timeframe when prophetic predictions will be realized. At the same time, it allows him to be sufficiently non-specific that his predictions do not become discredited.[44] Verse 25 concludes with a reference to "a time of distress." The Hebrew word translated here as "distress" is not common in the Hebrew Bible, but occurs in Deut 28:53, 55, 57. Deuteronomy 28 is a text that lists the blessings and the punishments attached to Israel's covenant with Yhwh. Among the threatened punishments is invasion by an enemy who lays siege to cities or towns. During such a disaster people will be driven to cannibalism because of "the distress with which your enemies will distress you" (Deut 28:53—RSV translation). The reference to "distress" in Dan 9:25 evokes the memory of what happened during the siege of Jerusalem in 587.[45] Verse 27 then predicts that seventy years of the

41. Collins, *Daniel*, 355; Goldingay, *Daniel*, 260–61.

42. For Collins, the word refers to v. 23 and the revelation there to Daniel (Collins, *Daniel*, 355). For Bergsma, the decree of Cyrus (Bergsma, "Daniel 9.1–27," 59).

43. So, Redditt, "Daniel 9: Its Structure and Meaning," 238–39; Seow, *Daniel*, 149–50.

44. As Redditt says of the author, "On the one hand he must point to a date, or a general span of time, when conditions will improve. On the other he must try to avoid being so specific that a delay in God's timing will undercut his prediction. The use of Sabbaths and Jubilees in Daniel 9 allowed its author to strike that balance" (Redditt, "Daniel 9: Its Structure and Meaning," 249).

45. The "time of distress" of 9:25 may also refer to Israel's history since the end of the

desolations of Jerusalem will be completed with the appearance and then demise of "the abomination that desolates," a reference to Antiochus IV and his desecration of the temple.[46]

Daniel 9 then addresses the question of the end of exile and the apparent non-fulfilment of Jeremiah's prophecy that Babylonian domination and the exile of Judeans would last seventy years. The figure of seventy years is reinterpreted to mean seventy weeks of years, or 490 years, a calculation based on Lev 25. Daniel 9 uses the idea of the exile in Babylon to describe the distress of the Jewish community of the Maccabean period, which consists of a) Judea under occupation by a foreign power, the Seleucids; b) their introduction of Hellenistic practices that are contrary to the Torah; c) the adoption of these practices by some of the Jewish community; d) the desecration of the Jerusalem temple by placing in it a cultic object, enigmatically referred to as "the abomination that desolates" (9:27).

According to Dan 9, Yhwh has decreed that there will be an end to exile, brought about by the action of Yhwh, "not because of the prayer or the repentance of the people."[47] The events that in v. 24 signal the end of the exile are both specific and vague. On the one hand, "To finish the transgression" is a reference to the behavior of Antiochus Epiphanes and his Jewish sympathizers. "To anoint a most holy place" refers to the cleansing and rededication of the Jerusalem temple. On the other hand, references to "put an end to sin," "to atone for iniquity," and "to bring in everlasting righteousness," vague in character, are in some way related to the crisis caused by Antiochus Epiphanes. The same can be said about other future happenings described in vv. 25–37. These vaguely described happenings are connected to the crisis of the second century BC, but their meaning transcends one historical situation.[48] The combination of the specific and the vague produces a tension in v. 27. Some of the signals that indicate the end of exile are relatively clear, and within a comprehensible timeframe, while other, more vague ones suggest that the end of the exile is nowhere in sight.

---

neo-Babylonian era as one of apostasy (Collins, *Daniel*, 356). Goldingay draws attention to the correct literal translation of בצוק העתים as "the trouble of the times" rather than "the times of trouble." He suggests v. 25b may refer to "the two features of the postexilic history that could be known from the OT, the rebuilding of the city and the pressure of Israel's hostile neighbours" (Goldingay, *Daniel*, 230).

46. The exact nature of the abomination has been disputed over many years. For a survey of interpretations see Collins, *Daniel*, 357–58.

47. Collins, *Daniel*, 360.

48. Goldingay, *Daniel*, 267.

In Dan 9 the vision of the future that will succeed the exile is not just expressed in terms of a restoration of past institutions and practices. The presence of apocalyptic language in the chapter means that the future is presented in a mysterious way, intelligible only to those who belong to an inner circle and understand the coded language. So, while the end of exile will bring about the restoration of the Jerusalem temple, other predictions of the future are shrouded in mystery. What is clear is that there will be an end to exile, but brought about only by the action of Yhwh, and not dependent on the prior repentance of people.

Daniel and the Unended Exile

The book of Daniel addressed the crisis of the Jewish community in the second century BCE when Judea was invaded by the Seleucids, Hellenistic practices contrary to the Torah were imposed, and the Jerusalem temple desecrated by Antiochus Epiphanes IV. The book addresses the crisis by situating narratives and visions in the time of the Babylonian occupation of Judah, and the exile of some of the population. The book uses the memory and experience of an event from the past to address and interpret a situation in the present. The book promises an end to exile and a future for the people. Included in its vision of the future are elements of restoration, namely the rebuilding and rededication of the Jerusalem temple. Other aspects of its future are expressed in apocalyptic language, the meaning of which is left unexplained.

THE BOOK OF BARUCH

Even clearer references to an unended exile can be found in the book of Baruch. Dates for the book's final form vary from the second century BCE to the mid-first century CE, but some of the book's material may come from a much earlier time.[49] The book refers to two groups of Israel—one living in Babylon as exiles from Judah, and the other in Jerusalem—but both communities are portrayed as still in exile.

The book's focus on exile is signalled at the very beginning. The book is attributed to Baruch ben Neriah, the scribe of the prophet Jeremiah, and so takes the reader back to the neo-Babylonian era. It also situates him in

---

49. So, J. Edward Wright, *Baruch*, 45.

Babylon, which is not a place where, according to the book of Jeremiah, Baruch ever went. It comes to us in Greek, but sections of it may have been written in Hebrew.[50] Since it contains some material also found in the book of Daniel, the earliest date for its composition is 165 BCE.[51] Its diction and theological outlook has been influenced by Deutero-Isaiah, the Deuteronomistic tradition, the book of Jeremiah, and the wisdom literature. It has four clearly defined parts, each of which may have existed as an independent text. The book consists of a narrative introduction (1:1–15a) and a book written by Baruch (1:15b—5:9), which has three distinct sections: a) a prayer of confession (1:15b—3:8); b) a wisdom text (3:9—4:4); c) a message of consolation (3:9—5:9).[52] Our focus here is on the final form of the text rather than the compositional history of the book's various sections.

A Book within a Book (1:1–15a)

The introduction (1:1–15a) has the effect of relating the different sections of the book, although originating in different historical periods, to the particular historical events indicated in vv. 1–3. The book of Baruch is a book that contains a book, as its superscription indicates: "These are the words of the book that Baruch . . . wrote" (1:1). The contents of this book are read firstly to the exiles in Babylon (v. 3), and it is then taken to Jerusalem to be read by the community there (v. 14).

The book begins by situating Baruch in Babylon (1:1). There he gathered the exiled king, Jeconiah (Jehoiachin), and all the deportees, and then read them words of a book that he had written (vv. 1–3). The reading took place "in the fifth year, on the seventh day of the month, at the time when the Chaldeans took Jerusalem and burned it with fire" (v. 2). The year in question is some time after 587 BCE, when the Jerusalem temple was razed by the Babylonians, "in the fifth month, on the seventh day" (2 Kgs 25:8). We are not yet told the contents of the letter, but the community's responses to it us a clue: "they wept, and fasted, and prayed before the Lord" (v. 5).

The situation of the exiles in Babylon is described in vv. 5–14a. Although in a foreign land, they are in contact with the community in Judah.

---

50. J. Edward Wright, *Baruch*, 47. See also Dimant, "From the Book of Jeremiah," 464–64; Nickelsburg, "The Bible Rewritten," 145.

51. J. Edward Wright, *Baruch*, 47.

52. The divisions of the book are generally agreed by scholars. See, e.g., Wacker, *Baruch*, 2–3; Nickelsburg, "The Bible Rewritten," 141–42; J. Edward Wright, *Baruch*, 46.

They have sufficient resources to raise money to pay for sin offerings at the Jerusalem temple (v. 10). Although they ask the Jerusalem community to pray for the Babylonian ruler Nebuchadnezzar and his son (vv. 11–12), the exiles live in Babylon under duress: Nebuchadnezzar "carried them away" (v. 9). The reason for their banishment is in v. 13: "We have sinned against the Lord our God, and to this day the anger of the Lord and his wrath have not turned away from us."

Now, while v. 13 expresses the conventional Deuteronomistic theology of exile as punishment for the people's sin, there is an important shift in focus in v. 14. Here the exiles exhort the Jerusalem community to "make your confession." The Greek verb used here and translated in the NRSV as "to confess," is most commonly followed by some reference to sin. It occurs in an exilic context in Lev 26:40.[53] Here Yhwh promises that if the survivors of the Babylonian conquest confess their sin and that of their ancestors, then he will remember his covenant and look favorably on them. Similarly, the Jerusalem community in the book of Baruch is also guilty and in need of forgiveness. It is important to note that when the community in Jerusalem is to read the letter of the exiles, they are directed to make confession for their own sins at the same time. Verse 14 reads "You shall read aloud this scroll . . . to make *your* confession." The Jerusalem community is not simply praying on behalf of that in Babylon, but is confessing its own failure. It is the prayer of both the exiles in Babylon and the community in Jerusalem. Both the Babylonian and Jerusalem communities are said to suffer "shame" (1:15; 2:6), a word used in texts in prophetic texts describing the condition of the people after the Babylonian destruction of Judah in 587.[54]

"See, we are today in our exile" (3:8)

The introduction is followed by a prayer of forgiveness, which extends from 1:15b to 3:8. It is framed in the first person plural, and so it becomes the prayer of both communities. The effect of using the first person plural is to unite both the community in Babylon and that in Jerusalem: "we" refers to

---

53. The Greek verb in question is ἐξαγορεύω. Texts in which it is followed by references to sin are Lev 5:5; Num 5:7; Neh 1:6; 9:2. It is not found in the Deuteronomistic literature.

54. The Greek word used here is αἰσχύνη, and is found in, e.g., Isa 54:4; Jer 2:26; Ezek 16:36, 37. See also Dan 9:7, where the people who are scattered by Yhwh are in a state of "open shame" (ἡ αἰσχύνη τοῦ προσωπου), the same expression as is in Bar 1:14).

them both. They are both equally as guilty of sin, and both share the same situation of alienation from Yhwh, which is expressed by the imagery of exile and diaspora.[55] Both are in exile. This is clearly true of the community in Babylon, but just as true of that in Jerusalem. The latter may be in their homeland, but according to their prayer, they are exiled and dispersed. The "we" of the prayer also refers to the Israel of the present, and also to the Israel of the past. The present distress of exile is Yhwh's punishment for the sins of the Israel of the present, as well as for the failings of the ancestors (1:19–21).[56]

The linking of the present to the past has the effect of prolonging the effects of the failures of the earlier generations. Exile, the punishment for the earlier generations' iniquity, has not ended but still continues. The present generation had sinned, but had also repented. Yet it still suffers for the evil of the past, as is evident in the concluding verses of the prayer:[57]

> For you have put the fear of you in our hearts so that we would call upon your name; and we will praise you in our exile, for we have put away from our hearts all the iniquity of our ancestors who sinned against you.
> See, we are today in our exile where you have scattered us, to be reproached and cursed and punished for all the iniquities of our ancestors, who forsook the Lord our God. (3:7–8)

These verses conclude the prayer of confession. Together with v. 5, these verses lay the blame for the community's present situation on the ancestors and their sins. According to v. 7, the sins of the ancestors weigh on the hearts of their descendants, an allusion to texts such as Jer 31:19–30 and Ezek 18:2, where the children complain that they have inherited the guilt of their ancestors.[58] The same sentiment is also in v. 8.

Verse 8 understands exile as something more all-embracing than banishment to Babylon. It situates the people in three different locations. There is the community in Jerusalem, the exiles in Babylon, and others scattered in diaspora. It is a rare occurrence in the Greek OT where the two words for

---

55. For a treatment of the whole prayer, see Wacker, *Baruch*, 15–37. For a more detailed and very comprehensive study see Steck, *Das apokryphe Baruchbuch*, 67–115.

56. For further see Steck, *Das apokryphe Baruchbuch*, 72–75.

57. The Greek word ἀποικία, translated by the NRSV and RSV as "exile" (v. 7) means "a settlement far from home." It is the usual word in the LXX to translate the Hebrew word for exile (גולה). For this, see Wacker, *Baruch*, 12.

58. So, Wacker, *Baruch*, 36.

exile and diaspora are brought together in one verse.[59] Here the presence of the two words suggests that exile and diaspora are interchangeable terms, as 2:29-32 also suggest. These verses are part of a historical retrospective in the prayer typical of the Deuteronomistic view of Israel's history. Disobedience to the Torah, as found in Deuteronomy, will lead to their banishment from the land with much of the population being wiped out, while survivors are scattered among the nations (Bar 2:29): "The LORD will scatter you among the peoples, only a few of you will be left" (Deut 4:29).

Following the prayer of confession are words of hope and encouragement that promise the end of exile (and diaspora) and a return to the homeland. 3:9—4:4 are a call to wisdom, which is equated with the Torah (4:1). Obedience to it is the key to Israel's future. The next section of the book, 4:5—5:9, consists of promises and consolation, most of which are spoken by Jerusalem, personified as Israel's mother (4:9a-37). 4:36-37 conclude the section with a summons to Jerusalem to look up and see the return of her children: "They are coming, gathered from east and west, at the word of the Holy One" (v. 37). The "gathering" is the opposite of "scattering." The use of the former is a signal that there will be an end to exile, and a scattered people will be brought back to their homeland.

5:1-9, addressed to the personified Jerusalem, conclude the book. Verse 5 is almost a verbatim repetition of the promise in v. 37. Together with 4:36-37, 5:1-9 pick up themes and images from Isa 40-55 and 56-66.[60] The word "glory" provides by far the most frequent intertextual link. The word occurs six times in Bar 5, ten in Isa 40-55, and fifteen in Isa 56-66. The gathering of Jerusalem's children in Bar 4:37 and 5:5 points back to a similar promises in Isa 43:5; 49:18. The flattening of hills and the filling in of the valleys, promised in Bar 5:7, points back to the similar imagery in Isa 40:4. The dialectic of Yhwh's forgetting and remembering his people can be seen in Bar 4:27; 5:5 and Isa 49:14. Jerusalem's promised splendor referred to in Bar 5:3 (also 4:24) is found in Isa 60:3. The changing of Jerusalem's garments of sorrow to those of joy, referred to in Bar 5:1, refers back to Isa 52:1; 61:10.

At first sight, one function of the links between Bar 5 and these Isaian texts is to create a sense of hope and great expectation that Yhwh has not forgotten Israel, and that the present distress will give way to a bright

---

59. Greek: ἰδοὺ ἡμεῖς σήμερον ἐν τῇ ἀποικίᾳ ἡμῶν οὗ διέσπειρας ἡμᾶς ἐκεῖ (3:8).

60. For an extensive list of the Isaian texts alluded to in Bar 5, see Steck, *Das apokryphe Baruchbuch*, 226-36.

future. However, the links to Isa 40–55 suggest something else. They take us back to the situation of the exiles in Babylon, and so the intended audience of the book of Baruch are portrayed as being in the same situation as the audience of Isa 40–55. Even though Baruch's audience are living in Jerusalem, they are in exile like their earlier ancestors in Babylon. Then the function of the links back to Isa 56–66 is to take us back to the Persian period, and to the disillusionment that is reflected in those chapters. The lyrical vision of a utopian future of Isa 40–55 was never realized. Instead there was a disillusioned and divided community. Would this also be the fate of the intended audience of Baruch?

The book of Baruch in its final form does not know of an end to exile. Its final chapter contains promises of a future, but beneath the surface of the text there is the tension between a vision of a marvelous future and its failure to be realized. It is the same tension that was present in the community in early Persian period in Yehud. The present is a situation of disillusionment and the community waits for the wonderful vision of a new exodus to be realized.

SUMMARY

The emergence of a belief in an unended exile can be seen in the texts studied in this chapter. In very different ways, Isa 56–66, Jeremiah MT, Daniel, and Baruch construct the idea of an unended exile. Isaiah 56–66 reflects on the non-fulfillment of the prophecies of a homecoming in chapters 40–55. They reflect the disillusionment of a section of the community living in early Persian-period Yehud. It describes the situation there in language that Isa 40–55 uses to describe that of the exiles in Babylon. Apart from geographical differences, life in Yehud for Isa 56–66 is no different to what was experienced in Babylon. The community was still in exile.

Jeremiah MT portrays the idea of an unended exile principally through the book's exilic frame and its construction of the figure of Babylon. Its exilic frame means that, although there are promises of deliverance and a return to the homeland, the book begins and ends in exile. It also portrays Babylon not just as a sixth-century historical nation, but as a trans-historical figure, whose demise will come after a period of seventy years. The book of Daniel takes up the Jeremian prediction about the seventy years of Babylonian domination followed by a return to the homeland. Daniel ponders over the prediction and realizes that it has not been fulfilled because of the people's sin. After he makes a prayer of confession on their behalf, he receives a promise that Jerusalem would be restored and rebuilt, and so the exile would come to an end at some indefinite time in the future.

Finally, the book of Baruch also portrays the exile as unended. It refers to communities in Babylon, in Jerusalem, and in diaspora, and understands them all to be in exile, even those in Jerusalem. The exile continues because of the sins of earlier generations. Even though the present generation had sinned but had then confessed its guilt, it still suffers because of the sins of the ancestors. The book concludes with the image of a beautifully clothed Jerusalem watching as her inhabitants get ready to return to the homeland. By the end of the book, we see that a homecoming is promised but not yet realized. The exile continues.

Chapter 7

CONCLUSION

By the late Second Temple period, a belief in an unended exile was an important concept in the Judaism of the time. Having traced the development of this idea in the preceding chapters, we are now better able to appreciate the discussion about the role of the unended exile in the New Testament, especially in the writings of N. T. Wright. However, a summary of the preceding chapters and what they have brought to light is in order.

SUMMARY OF CHAPTERS 2-3

The preceding chapters have shown how the experience of an elite group of Judahites of being exiled to Babylon in the sixth century BCE has become a paradigm that later generations used to interpret the events in their own particular historical periods. The experience of exile confronted both the deportees and also those left behind in Judah with fundamental questions about their faith, identity, and future.

Their crisis of faith was brought about by the Babylonian conquest of Judah, and the deportees' experience of Babylon, a city of far greater magnificence than Jerusalem. The Babylonian conquest and the magnificence of the city of Babylon indicated that their deities were far superior to Yhwh, who seemed impotent in comparison. Their identity crisis was brought about by their experience of living in this foreign land and culture. Some assimilated into the surrounding Babylonian culture, while others drew on Judah's sacred traditions to develop an identity built around the ideas of difference and separation. They developed identity markers such as the sabbath, circumcision, and distinctive dietary practices. They developed the older traditions about Abraham and the possession of Canaan, and saw themselves as the inheritors of the promise that his descendants would possess the land. A return to Judah was also central in Isa 40–55, which predicted a glorious return to the land that would far outweigh the splendor of the exodus from Egypt.

It was not until Cyrus II captured Babylon in 539 BCE that a return to the land was possible. However, by this stage most of the deportees from 597, 587, and 582 would have died. Instead of imagining that those deported were now able to just return home, we realize that we are dealing with the idea of a migration from Babylon to Judah (now the Persian province of Yehud). From a historical point of view, any large-scale migration, such as that described in Ezra 2, would not have been possible in the years immediately after 539 because of the instability that existed in Persia's empire during these years.

The book of Ezra gives a detailed description of how "returning exiles" made the journey from Babylon to Yehud. Its first few chapters situate the return shortly after Cyrus' defeat of Babylon, and they portray his conquest as marking the end of exile. However, although the book situates itself in the early years of the Persian period, it is in fact a later composition and it deals with issues of identity, inclusion, and exclusion in the Yehud of the fifth century BCE. In Ezra, both exile and restoration are constructs that advance the theological agenda of its composers. It is noteworthy that texts such as Haggai and Zech 1–8, which are compositions from the late sixth century, have either very little or no interest in the exile. They do speak of a restoration, but not one founded on exiles returning from Babylon.

A very different view about exile is found in Isa 56–66. Originating in Yehud in the early Persian period, the intended audience of these chapters are the inheritors of the promises of a wondrous deliverance and rebuilding found in chapters 40–55. The community reflected in Isa 56–66 are disillusioned. Instead of experiencing the fulfillment of the promises of a glorious homecoming and restoration, the community struggled with internal divisions, and the disillusionment about the failure of the promises to be realized. The same cry of abandonment that concluded the book of Lamentations (5:22) is also found in Isa 64:12. The uncertainty about Yhwh's intentions in Lam 5:22 still remained years later. In Isa 56–66, the promises of a new future found in chapters 40–55 are revisited, but the conclusion is clearly drawn that they have not been realized. The situation of the community in chapters 56–66 is expressed in the same language as that used of the exiles in Babylon in chapters 40–55. Little or nothing has changed. Life in the homeland and life in exile in Babylon morph into one experience of alienation. Living in the homeland, they continue to be in exile.

The book of Jeremiah MT, which reached its final form in the Persian period at the earliest, also portrays the exile as unended. It takes the historical figures of the Babylon of Nebuchadnezzar's era and develops it into a construct that transcends space and time. Babylon becomes Sheschach, a figure of mystery, whose power still continues (25:15–26). The book predicts an end to exile, but in its narrative world, this lies in the yet-to-be realized future. The mythic portrait of Babylon is also shown by the book's construction of the figure of Nebuchadnezzar. Although the leader of an army that conquered and destroyed Jerusalem and its temple, he is referred to as Yhwh's servant (25:9), which elevates him to a status shared only by figures like Abraham, Moses, and David.

Jeremiah MT is also framed by references to exile. Its superscription describes the mission of Jeremiah as extending from 627 down to 587 BCE, although the book's contents refer to events after that year. It ends with an account of the siege and downfall of Jerusalem in 587, and a reference to Jehoiachin as a prisoner in Babylon. So, Jeremiah MT begins and ends in exile. It does predict an end to exile, but this promise is not realized in the book.

Like Jeremiah MT, the book of Daniel portrays the exile unended. Although it reached its final form in the Maccabean era, Daniel too opens with references to exile. Its early chapters are set in the reign of Nebuchadnezzar. Daniel and his three companions, deported from Judah, are servants in the emperor's court in Babylon (Dan 1–4). Although the book portrays that the Babylonian domination has been supplanted by the Persian Empire, Daniel still remains in exile. According to chapter 9, Daniel is troubled by the situation of the Jewish community of his time. He understands that their present distress ("the devastation of Jerusalem"—9:2) was brought about by their sinfulness. In response to his prayer of confession and plea for forgiveness (9:5–11), the angel Gabriel provides an interpretation of the seventy years as a symbolic figure, the precise meaning of which is not revealed. What is clear from the book is that, at its end, the seventy years has not been completed, and that the "devastations of Jerusalem," and therefore the exile, has not yet come to an end.

The book of Baruch also portrays the exile as unended. In it, the people of Israel are portrayed in three different situations. There is a community in Babylon, another in Jerusalem, and a further group who are scattered among different nations. What unites them is that they are all in exile. The cause of their exile is either the sins of their own generation or that of their ancestors. Much of the book consists of a long prayer of penitence (1:15—3:8), which is heavily influenced by Deuteronomistic theology. The present distress is understood as Yhwh's punishment for the people's sin. The confession of sin opens the way for Yhwh to forgive them and bring them to the homeland. The last section of the book (5:1–8) uses imagery from Isa 40–55 to hold out the hope of a wonderful future. Read at one level, it offers hope that Yhwh will gather Jerusalem's children "from west and east" (5:5) and bring them home. However, read at another level, the use the Isaian imagery from chapters 40–55 situates the intended audience back to the time of the sixth-century community in Babylon who first heard the message of a joyful and splendid return to the homeland. We are left with an unanswered question. Such a return was not realized for the sixth-century exiles in Babylon—will it be realized for the intended audience of Baruch centuries later?

The Unended Exile: Christian Gospels and Early CE Judaism

The significance of an unended exile for the New Testament has become a much debated topics. Its prime protagonist has been the British scholar N. T. Wright, who has argued that in the time of Jesus "Exile and restoration was the central drama that Israel believed itself to be acting out."[1] He also saw this idea as central to the writings of Paul.[2] Exile and restoration formed the great meta-narrative under which were gathered other OT traditions.

His position has been criticized as too all-embracing.[3] While this may be true, the previous chapters in this book have shown that the idea of

---

1. N. T. Wright, "Yet the Sun Will Rise Again," 45; also N. T. Wright, *Jesus and the Victory of God*, 126–29.

2. "For Paul, the period of the exile ended in Christ" (N. T. Wright, "Yet the Sun Will Rise Again," 62).

3. See, e.g., Pitre, *Jesus*, 31–40. He argues that Wright is correct in focussing on the idea of exile as an overarching theme, but maintains he is wrong in identifying the exile with that of Judah in the neo-Babylonian period. Pitre believes that the unended exile in the OT is about the tribes of the Northern Kingdom. Restoration will come about when the twelve tribes are brought back to the land.

CONCLUSION

an unended exile was clearly one element in Judaism's self-understanding in the late Second Temple period. It was also carried over at least in the New Testament's Synoptic Gospels. As a way of concluding this book, I want to briefly point out some Gospel texts that reflect the idea of an unended exile. I do not intend to rehearse arguments already made by other scholars. Rather, I want to single out a couple of texts that, as far as I can see, have not figured much in discussions about exilic imagery in the Gospels.

The three Synoptic Gospels all record the appearance and preaching of John the Baptist as the prelude to the ministry of Jesus. Where John is introduced in all three, a text from the book of Isaiah is quoted: "prepare the way of the Lord, make his paths straight" (Matt 3:3; Mark 1:3; Luke 3:4; cf. Isa 40:3). The presence of these Isaian references in the three Synoptics and their similar portraits of John would indicate that we are dealing with a tradition that reflects an early stage in the formation of the Gospels. What is significant is that the Isaian quotes appears at the beginning of Isaiah 40–55. Used in the Synoptics, its rhetorical effect is to take the reader back to the time of the exiles in Babylon. The promises made them are now applied to the later situation. The intended audience of the Gospel tradition understands itself as being in exile, and awaiting a homecoming that will be brought about by the ministry of Jesus.

Another text that signals that the idea of exile is important in the Gospels is the genealogy of Jesus in Matthew. It constructs a genealogy of forty-two generations, which are divided into three sections of fourteen. The genealogy begins with Abraham (Matt 1:2). The first fourteen generations conclude with David (1:6), the second fourteen with the deportation to Babylon (v. 11), and the third with Jesus (v. 16). The text then emphasizes how each set of fourteen generations concludes:

> So all the generations from Abraham to David are fourteen generations; and from David to the deportation to Babylon, fourteen generations; and from the deportation to Babylon to the Messiah, fourteen generations (1:17).

In interpreting the genealogy, scholars of Matthew's Gospel have usually emphasized the beginning and ending of the first set of the generations and the ending of the third. They propose that the genealogy foreshadows key ideas in this gospel, such as Jesus' descent from Abraham, his roles as the son of David and messiah. There is usually very little comment on the end of the second set of the generations, and its significance for Matthew's

Gospel.⁴ If the end of the first set provides an critical interpretive key to the Gospel, surely the end of the second also has the same force: the idea of exile must also be a key to understanding Matthew's story.

There is also exilic imagery in the Gospel of Luke.⁵ The placing of John the Baptist in the wilderness is an allusion back to the generation led by Moses to the promised land.⁶ Similarly the use of Isa 40:3 to describe John's ministry takes the reader back to the promises in Isa 56–66 about a restoration to the land.⁷ Another key text is the narrative of Jesus in the synagogue at Nazareth. He reads from Isa 61:1. It takes the Gospel's audience back to the community in the early Persian period. They were a disillusioned and divided people, wondering when the promises of a wonderful return to the homeland would be realized. For the audience of Luke's Gospel, the end of exile was about to happen by means of the ministry of Jesus.⁸ Isaiah 61:1 is also quoted in a relevant text from Matthew (11:1–6), where John's disciples ask Jesus about his identity. His reply is to quote Isa 61:1. His mission, in which he heals the blind, deaf, lame, and lepers, marks the end of the exile.

Imagery associated with exile was also used in Judaism to describe the destruction of the Jerusalem temple in 70 CE and its aftermath. The figures of the prophet Jeremiah and Baruch and the events of 587 were used to describe the Roman action.⁹ Second Baruch, also known as *The Syriac Apocalypse*, was a reflection on the events of 70 CE, but situates itself in the neo-Babylonian era. It begins: "And it came to pass in the twenty-ninth year of Jeconiah, king of Judah" (1:1).¹⁰ According to 2 Baruch, Jer-

---

4. One exception is Piotrowski, who calls the period from the Babylonian exile to the time of Jesus an "unending exile" (Piotrowski, *Matthew's New David*, 36). The coming of Jesus means that "the end of exile is now in view" (Piotrowski, *Matthew's New David*, 36–37). There are also some similar, but briefer comments in McKnight, "Exiled to the Land," 204.

5. For Luke's understanding of Israel's exile, see Fuller, *The Restoration of Israel*, 211–37.

6. Fuller, *The Restoration of Israel*, 211–12.

7. Fuller, *The Restoration of Israel*, 212.

8. Fuller, *The Restoration of Israel*, 236–39. There is also a small but significant allusion to the end of exile is found in Luke 2:25, which refers to Simeon as "looking forward to the consolation (παράκλησις) of Israel." The noun παράκλησις is derived from the verb παρακαλέω, which forms the first words of Isa 40:1 LXX: παρακαλεῖτε παρακαλεῖτε τον λαον μου ("comfort, comfort my people"). Simeon was patiently waiting for the end of exile.

9. Kipp Davis, "Prophets of Exile," 497–99.

10. On 2 Baruch, see J. Edward Wright, *Baruch*, 75. For a full treatment, see Nir, *The Destruction of Jerusalem*. Other texts that similarly refer to the events of 587 are e.g., *The Paralipomena of Jeremiah*, *4 Ezra*, and the much disputed *3 Baruch*.

emiah accompanies the exiles to Babylon, while Baruch himself remains in Jerusalem (9:1).

EXILE: FROM HISTORICAL EVENT TO BIBLICAL PARADIGM

This book's study of exile started with the invasion of Judah in 587 BCE and the deportation of a segment of its population to Babylon. We then explored how these events were interpreted in the Old Testament. We first saw that they were interpreted as divine punishment for the nation's sin. It was accompanied by grief, disillusionment, struggles about faith, and questions about whether there was future for the community. We then noted that there were significant changes in how the events were interpreted. One change was in the attitude of the deportees about living in Babylon. The letter of Jeremiah encouraged them to look on the place of their exile as their new home. It would even supplant Jerusalem. Another significant change was in the book of Ezra, where being an exile became a marker, which separated the true Israelite from someone who did not belong. We further saw that in the early Persian period life in Yehud was described in terms similar to those used about life in exile. Evidence for this was found in Isa 56–66. The idea of exile was separated from its geographical moorings, and became a metaphor for describing and interpreting what was wrong with the community. Later literature, such as the book of Jeremiah MT, then portrayed the exile as still continuing. The question that then arose was about when the exile would end, an issue pursued in Dan 9. Our reading of the book of Baruch confirmed that in the late Second Temple period there was the belief that the exile still continued and had not yet come to an end.

The process we have followed in this study is one whereby a historical event became a paradigm. What characterizes a paradigm is that it "consists of generalizations concerning the human situation, patterns of conduct and consequence, and the paradigm governs present and past without distinction."[11] So, as a biblical paradigm, the imagery of exile reappears in traditions composed well after 587. The paradigm of the exile, founded on the events of 587 and their aftermath, provided the Judaism of the early Common Era with a way of comprehending and interpreting what happened in 70 CE.[12] As time went on texts such as Lamentations Rabbah and

11. Neusner, "The Idea of History," 278.
12. See Neusner, "The Idea of History," 288–91.

the Targum of Lamentations appeared. They were commentaries on the book of Lamentations, and used that text to reflect on the events of the year 70 CE. Their meaning was explained by reading and commenting on a text from the neo-Babylonian era.

Today, exile is still a powerful paradigm to describe the experience of individuals or communities when their fundamental value systems collapse. The biblical paradigm provides a way of resolving issues that accompany the collapse, such as grief, disillusionment, despair about a future, and a loss of faith. The paradigm has retained its power and relevance over the centuries because it is an expression of reality. It does not deny the pain and the horror of what might have occurred, but at the same time still holds forth the hope that a new future can emerge from the wreckage of the present.

BIBLIOGRAPHY

Abraham, Kathleen. "West Semitic and Judean Brides in Cuneiform Sources from the Sixth Century BCE: New Evidence from a Marriage Contract from Āl-Yahudu." *AfO* 51 (2005/2006) 198–219.

Abruyten, Seth. "Pollution–Purification Rituals, Cultural Memory and the Evolution of Religion: How Collective Trauma Shaped Ancient Israel." *American Journal of Cultural Sociology* 3 (2015) 123–55.

Ackroyd, Peter R. *Exile and Restoration: A Study of Hebrew Thought in the Sixth Century BC.* London: SCM, 1968.

Ahn, John J. *Exile as Forced Migrations: A Sociological, Literary, and Theological Approach on the Displacement and Resettlement of the Southern Kingdom of Judah.* BZAW 417. Berlin: De Gruyter, 2011.

Ahn, John J., and Jill Middlemas, eds. *By the Irrigation Canals of Babylon: Approaches to the Study of the Exile.* LHBOTS 526. New York: Continuum, 2012.

Albertz, Rainer. *A History of Israelite Religion in the Old Testament Period. Volume 2: From the Exile to the Maccabees.* London: SCM, 1994.

———. *Israel in Exile: The History and Literature of the Sixth Century B.C.E.* SBL Studies in Biblical Literature 3. Atlanta: SBL, 2003.

Albertz, Rainer, and Bob Becking, eds. *Yahwism After the Exile: Perspectives on Israelite Religion in the Persian Era.* STAR 5. Assen: Royal Van Gorcum, 2003.

Albright, W. F. *The Archaeology of Palestine.* Mitcham, Australia: Penguin, 1961.

Allen, Leslie C. *Ezekiel 1–19.* WBC 28. Dallas: Word, 1994.

———. *Ezekiel 20–48.* WBC 29. Dallas: Word, 1990.

———. *Jeremiah: A Commentary.* OTL. Louisville: Westminster John Knox, 2008.

———. "The Structuring of Ezekiel's Revisionist History." *CBQ* 54 (1992) 448–62.

Ames, Frank Ritchel. "The Cascading Effects of Exile: From Diminished Resources to New Identities." In *Interpreting Exile: Displacement and Deportation in Biblical and Modern Context*, edited by Brad E. Kelle, Frank Ritchel Ames, and Jacob L. Wright, 173–87. Ancient Israel and Its Literature 12. Atlanta: SBL, 2011.

Amzallag, Nissim. "The Authorship of Ezra and Nehemiah in Light of Differences in Their Ideological Background." *JBL* 137 (2018) 271–97.

Apóstolo, Silvio. "Imagining Ezekiel." *JHS* 8, article 13 (2008) 2–30.

Assis, Elie. "The Alphabetic Acrostic in the Book of Lamentations." *CBQ* 69 (2007) 710–24.

Baltzar, Klaus. *Deutero-Isaiah: A Commentary on Isaiah 40—55.* Hermeneia. Minneapolis: Fortress, 2001.

BIBLIOGRAPHY

Barstad, Hans M. "After the 'Myth of the Empty Land': Major Challenges in the Study of Neo-Babylonian Judah." In *Judah and the Judeans in the Neo-Babylonian Period*, edited by Oded Lipschits and Joseph Blenkinsopp, 3–20. Winona Lake, IN: Eisenbrauns, 2003.

———. "The Myth of the Empty Land: A Study in the History and Archaeology of Judah During the 'Exilic' Period." In *The Myth of the Empty Land: A Study in the History and Archaeology of Judah During the "Exilic" Period*. SO 28. Oslo: Scandinavian University Press, 1996.

Bauks, Michaela. "Die Begriffe מוֹרָשָׁה und אֲחֻזָּה in Pg Überlegungen zur Landkonzeption der Priestergrundschrift." *ZAW* 116 (2004) 1–18.

Bautch, Richard J. *Developments in Genre Between Post-Exilic Penitential Prayers and the Psalms of Communal Lament*. Atlanta: SBL, 2003.

Beaulieu, Paul-Aland. "Yahwistic Names in Light of Late Babylonian Onomastics." In *Judah and the Judeans in the Achaemenid Period*, edited by Oded Lipschits, Gary N. Knopper, and Manfred Oeming, 249–54. Winona Lake, IN: Eisenbrauns, 2011.

Becking, Bob. "'We All Returned as One': Critical Notes on the Myth of the Mass Return." In *Judah and the Judeans in the Persian Period*, edited by Oded Lipschits and Joseph Blenkinsopp, 3–18. Winona Lake, IN: Eisenbrauns, 2006.

Bedford, Peter R. *Temple Restoration in Early Achaemenid Judah*. JSJSup 65. Leiden: Brill, 2000.

Ben Zvi, Ehud. "Total Exile, Empty Land and the General Intellectual Discourse in Yehud." In *The Concept of Exile in Ancient Israel and Its Historical Contexts*, edited by Ehud Ben Zvi and Christoph Levin, 155–68. BZAW 404. Berlin: De Gruyter, 2010.

———. "What Is New in Yehud? Some Considerations." In *Yahwism After the Exile: Perspectives on Israelite Religion in the Persian Era*, edited by Rainer Albertz and Bob Becking, 32–48. Assen: Royal Van Gorcum, 2003.

Ben Zvi, Ehud, and Christoph Levin, eds. *The Concept of Exile in Ancient Israel and Its Historical Contexts*. BZAW 404. Berlin: De Gruyter, 2010.

Bergsma, John S. "The Persian Period as Penitential Era: The 'Exegetical Logic' of Daniel 9.1–27." In *Exile and Restoration Revisited: Essays on the Babylonian and Persian Periods in Memory of Peter R. Ackroyd*, edited by Gary N. Knoppers, Lester L. Grabbe, and Deirdre Fulton, 50–64. LSTS 73. London: T. & T. Clark, 2009.

Berlin, Adele. *Lamentations*. OTL. Louisville: Westminster John Knox, 2002.

———. "On Writing a Commentary on Lamentations." In *Lamentations in Ancient and Contemporary Cultural Contexts*, edited by Nancy C. Lee and Carleen Mandolfo, 3–11. SBL Symposium Series 43. Atlanta: SBL, 2008.

Berquist, Jon L. *Approaching Yehud: New Approaches to the Study of the Pentateuch*. SBL Semitic Studies 50. Atlanta: SBL, 2007.

Betylon, John W. "Neo-Babylonian Military Operations Other Than War in Judah and Jerusalem." In *Judah and the Judeans in the Neo-Babylonian Period*, edited by Oded Lipschits and Joseph Blenkinsopp, 263–83. Winona Lake, IN: Eisenbrauns, 2003.

———. "Palestine in the Persian Period." *Near Eastern Archaeology* 68 (2005) 4–58.

Bier, Miriam J. *"Perhaps There is Hope": Reading Lamentations as a Polyphony of Pain, Penitence, and Protest*. LHBOTS 603. London: Bloomsbury T. & T. Clark, 2015.

Blenkinsopp, Joseph. "The Bible, Archaeology and Politics; or The Empty Land Revisited." *JSOT* 27 (2002) 169–87.

———. *Ezra-Nehemiah*. OTL. London: SCM, 1989.

———. *Isaiah 40-55: A New Translation with Introduction and Commentary*. AB 19A. New York: Doubleday, 2002.

———. *Isaiah 56—66: A New Translation with Introduction and Commentary*. AB 19B. New York: Doubleday, 2003.

Block, Daniel I. *The Book of Ezekiel: Chapters 1-24*. NICOT. Grand Rapids: Eerdmans, 1997.

Boase, Elizabeth. "The Characterisation of God in Lamentations." *ABR* 56 (2008) 32-44.

Boda, Mark J. *The Book of Zechariah*. NICOT. Grand Rapids: Eerdmans, 2016.

———. "Scat! Exilic Motifs in the Book of Zechariah." In *The Prophets Speak on Forced Migration*, edited by Mark J. Boda, Frank Ritchel Ames, John Ahn, and Mark Leuchter, 161-80. SBL Ancient Israel and Its Literature 21. Atlanta: SBL, 2015.

———. "Terrifying the Horns: Persia and Babylon in Zechariah 1:7—6:15." *CBQ* 67 (2005) 22-41.

Boda, Mark J., Frank Ritchel Ames, John Ahn, and Mark Leuchter, eds. *The Prophets Speak on Forced Migration*. SBL Ancient Israel and Its Literature 21. Atlanta: SBL, 2015.

Boorer, Suzanne. *The Vision of the Priestly Narrative: Its Genre and Hermeneutics of Time*. Atlanta: SBL, 2016.

Brettler, Marc Zvi. "Judaism in the Hebrew Bible? The Transition from Ancient Israelite Religion to Judaism." *CBQ* 61 (1999) 429-47.

Briant, Pierre. *From Cyrus to Alexander: A History of the Persian Empire*. Winona Lake, IN: Eisenbrauns, 2002.

Bright, John. *A History of Israel*. 2nd ed. OTL. London: SCM, 1972.

Brueggemann, Walter. "Israel's Sense of Place in Jeremiah." In *Rhetorical Criticism*, edited by J. Jackson and M. Kessler, 149-65. Pittsburg, 1974.

Campbell, Antony F., and Mark A. O'Brien. *Unfolding the Deuteronomistic History: Origins, Upgrades, Present Text*. Minneapolis: Fortress, 2000.

Carroll, Robert P. *Jeremiah*. OTL. Philadelphia: Westminster, 1986.

———. "The Myth of the Empty Land." *Semeia* 59 (1992) 79-93.

Childs, Brevard S. *Exodus*. OTL. Louisville: Westminster, 1974.

———. *Isaiah: A Commentary*. OTL. Louisville: Westminster John Knox, 2001.

Clements, R. E. *God and Temple: The Idea of the Divine Presence in Ancient Israel*. Oxford: Blackwell, 1965.

Collins, John J. *Daniel: A Commentary on the Book of Daniel*. Hermeneia. Minneapolis: Fortress, 1993.

Conrad, Edgar W. *Zechariah*. Readings: A New Biblical Commentary. Sheffield, UK: Sheffield Academic, 1999.

Craigie, Peter C., Page H. Kelley, and Joel F. Drinkard Jr. *Jeremiah 1-25*. WBC 26. Dallas: Word, 1991.

Cross, Frank Moore. *Canaanite Myth and Hebrew Epic: Essays in the History of the Religion of Israel*. Cambridge: Harvard University Press, 1973.

Dandamayev, M. A. "Neo-Babylonian and Achaemenid State Administration in Mesopotamia." In *Judah and the Judeans in the Persian Period*, edited by Oded Lipschits and Manfred Oeming, 373-98. Winona Lake, IN: Eisenbrauns, 2006.

Davies, Philip R. "Exile? What Exile? Whose Exile?" In *Leading Captivity Captive: "The Exile" as History and Ideology*, edited by Lester L. Grabbe, 128-38. JSOTSup 278. Sheffield, UK: Sheffield Academic, 1998.

Davis, Ellen F. *Swallowing the Scroll: Textuality and the Dynamics of Discourse in Ezekiel's Prophecy*. JSOTSup 78. Sheffield, UK: Almond, 1989.

Davis, Kipp. "Prophets of Exile: '4QApocryphon of Jeremiah C', Apocryphal Baruch, and the Efficacy of the Second Temple." *JSJ* 44 (2013) 497–529.

Delorme, Jean-Philippe. "לארשי תיב In Ezekiel: Identity Construction and the Exilic Period." *JBL* 138 (2019) 121–41.

Dimant, Devorah. "From the Book of Jeremiah to the Qumranic 'Apocryphon of Jeremiah'." *DSD* 20 (2013) 452–71.

Dobbs-Allsopp, F. W. *Weep, O Daughter of Zion: A Study of the City-Lament Genre in the Hebrew Bible*. BibOr 44. Rome: Editrice Pontificio Istituto Biblico, 1993.

Douglas, Mary. "Responding to Ezra: The Priests and the Foreign Wives." *BibInt* 10 (2002) 2–23.

Duggan, Michael W. *The Covenant Renewal in Ezra-Nehemiah (Neh 7:72B—10:40) An Exegetical, Literary and Theological Study*. SBLDS 164. Atlanta: SBL, 2001.

Duhm, Bernhard. *Das Buch Jeremia*. Kurzer Hand-Commentar zum Alten Testament XI. Tübingen: Mohr [Siebeck], 1901.

Ehrlich, Carl S. "Ezekiel: The Prophet, His Times, His Message." *European Judaism* 32 (1999) 117–31.

Faust, Avraham. "The Bible, Archaeology, and the Practice of Circumcision in Israelite and Philistine Societies." *JBL* 134 (2015) 273–90.

———. *Judah in the Neo-Babylonian Period: The Archaeology of Desolation*. SBLABS 18. Atlanta: SBL, 2012.

Fishbane, Michael. *Biblical Interpretation in Ancient Israel*. Oxford: Clarendon, 1991.

Foster, R. S. *The Restoration of Israel: The Return from the Exile*. London: Darton, Longman and Todd, 1970.

Fried, Lisbeth S. *The Priest and the Great King: Temple-Palace Relations in the Persian Empire*. Biblical and Judaic Studies 10. Winona Lake, IN: Eisenbrauns, 2004.

Fritz, Volkmar. *1 & 2 Kings: A Continental Commentary*. Minneapolis: Fortress, 2003.

Fuller, Michael E. *The Restoration of Israel: Israel's Re-Gathering and the Fate of the Nations in Early Jewish Literature and Luke-Acts*. BNZW 138. Berlin: De Gruyter, 2006.

Galambush, Julie. *Jerusalem in the Book of Ezekiel: The City as Yahweh's Wife*. SBLDS 130. Atlanta: Scholars, 1992.

Gerstenberger, Erhard S. *Israel in the Persian Period: The Fifth and Fourth Centuries B.C.E.* SBL Biblical Enclyopedia Series 8. Atlanta: SBL, 2011.

Gesundheit, Shimon. "The Question of LXX Jeremiah as a Tool for Literary-Critical Analysis." *VT* 62 (2012) 29–57.

Goldingay, John E. *Daniel*. WBC 30. Dallas: Word, 1989.

Goldman, Yohanan. *Prophétie et royauté au retour de l'exil: les origines littéraires de la forme massorétique de livre de Jérémie*. OBO 118. Göttingen: Vandenhoeck & Ruprecht, 1992.

Gregory, Bradley C. "The Postexilic Exile in Third Isaiah: Isaiah 61:1–3 in Light of Second Temple Hermeneutics." *JBL* 126 (2007) 475–96.

Grünwaldt, Klaus. *Exil und Identität: Beschneidung, Passa und Sabbat in der Priesterschrift*. BBB. Frankfurt am Main: Anton Hain, 1992.

Hahn, Scott Walker, and John Sietze Bergsma. "What Laws Were 'Not Good'? A Canonical Approach to the Theological Problem of Ezekiel 20:25–26." *JBL* 123 (2004) 201–18.

Halpern, Baruch. "Why Manasseh Is Blamed for the Babylonian Exile: The Evolution of a Biblical Tradition." *VT* 48 (1998) 473–514.

Halvorson-Taylor, Martien A. *Enduring Exile: The Metaphorization of Exile in the Hebrew Bible*. VTS 141. Leiden: Brill, 2011.

Harris, Beau, and Carleen Mandolfo. "The Silent God in Lamentations." *Int* 67 (2013) 133–43.
Hayes, John H., and J.Maxwell Miller. *Israelite and Judean History*. OTL. London: SCM, 1977.
Hiebel, Janina Maria. *Ezekiel's Vision Accounts as Interrelated Narratives: A Redaction-Critical and Theological Study*. BZAW 475. Berlin: De Gruyter, 2015.
———. "Visions of Death and Re-Creation: Ezekiel 8–11 and 37:1–14 and the Crisis of Identity in the Babylon Exile and Beyond." *Pacifica* 28 (2015) 243–55.
Hill, John. *Friend or Foe? The Figure of Babylon in the Book of Jeremiah MT*. BIS 40. Leiden: Brill, 1999.
———. "Jeremiah 40.1–6: An Appreciation." In *Seeing Signals, Reading Signs: The Art of Exegesis. Studies in Honour of Antony F. Campbell, SJ for His Seventieth Birthday*, edited by Mark A. O'Brien and Howard N. Wallace, 130–41. London: T. & T. Clark, 2004.
———. "Writing the Prophetic Word—The Production of the Book of Jeremiah." *ABR* 57 (2009) 22–33.
———. "'Your Exile Will Be Long': The Book of Jeremiah and the Unended Exile." In *Reading the Book of Jeremiah: A Search for Coherence*, edited by Martin A. Kessler, 149–61. Winona Lake, IN: Eisenbrauns, 2004.
Holladay, William L. *Jeremiah 2: A Commentary on the Book of Jeremiah Chapters 26–52*. Hermeneia. Philadelphia: Fortress, 1989.
Janzen, David. *Witch-Hunts, Purity and Social Boundaries: The Expulsion of the Foreign Women in Ezra 9–10*. JSOTSup 350. Sheffield, UK: Sheffield Academic, 2002.
———. "Yahwistic Appropriation of Achaemenid Ideology and the Function of Nehemiah 9 in Ezra-Nehemiah." *JBL* 136 (2017) 839–56.
Japhet, Sara. *From the Rivers of Babylon to the Highlands of Judah: Collected Studies on the Restoration Period*. Winona Lake, IN: Eisenbrauns, 2006.
Joüon, Paul. *Grammar of Biblical Hebrew*. Subsidia Biblica 14/I. Rome: Pontificio Istituto Biblico, 1993.
Joyce, Paul M. *Divine Initiative and Human Response in Ezekiel*. JSOTSup 51. Sheffield, UK: JSOT, 1989.
———. *Ezekiel: A Commentary*. LHBOTS 482. London: T. & T. Clark, 2007.
Kelle, Brad E. "Dealing with the Trauma of Defeat: The Rhetoric of the Devastation and Rejuvenation of Nature in Ezekiel." *JBL* 128 (2009) 469–90.
Kelle, Brad E., Frank Ritchel Ames, and Jacob L. Wright, eds. *Interpreting Exile: Displacement and Deportation in Biblical and Modern Context*. Ancient Israel and Its Literature 12. Atlanta, Georgia: SBL, 2011.
Keown, Gerald L., Pamela J. Scalise, and Thomas G. Smothers. *Jeremiah 26–52*. WBC 27. Dallas: Word, 1995.
Kessler, John. "Diaspora and Homeland in the Early Achaemenid Period: Community, Geography and Demography in Zechariah 1–8." In *Approaching Yehud: New Approaches to the Study of the Pentateuch*, edited by Jon L. Berquist, 137–66. SBL Semitic Studies 50. Atlanta: SBL, 2007.
Kirkpatrick, Shane. *Competing for Honor: A Social-Scientific Reading of Daniel 1–6*. BIS 74. Leiden: Brill, 2005.
Klein, Anja. "Salvation for Sheep and Bones: Ezek 34 and 37 as Corner Pillars of Ezekiel's Prophecy of Salvation." In *Ezekiel: Current Debates and Future Directions*, edited by

William Tooman and Penelope Barter, 179–93. FAT 112. Tübingen: Mohr Siebeck, 2017.

Knoppers, Gary N. "The Construction of the Judean Diasporic Identity in Ezra-Nehemiah." *JHS* 15 (2015) article 3. Http://www.jhsonline.org/Articles/article_206.pdf.http://www.jhsonline.org/Articles/article_206.pdf.

———. "Prayer and Propaganda: Solomon's Dedication of the Temple and the Deuteronomist's Program." In *Reconsidering Israel and Judah: Recent Studies on the Deuteronomistic History*, edited by Gary N. Knoppers and J. Gordon McConville, 370–96. Sources for Biblical and Theological Study 8. Winona Lake, IN: Eisenbrauns, 2000.

Knoppers, Gary N., Lester L. Grabbe, and Deirdre Fulton, eds. *Exile and Restoration Revisited: Essays on the Babylonian and Persian Periods in Memory of Peter R. Ackroyd*. LSTS 73. London: T. & T. Clark, 2009.

Koch, Klaus. *Daniel*. BKAT 22/1. Neukirchen-Vluyn: Neukirchener Verlag, 2005.

Körting, Corinna. "Sach 5,5–11—Die Unrechtmäßigkeit wird an ihren Ort verwiesen." *Bib* 87 (2006) 477–92.

Kratz, Reinhard. "The Visions of Daniel." In *The Book of Daniel*, vol. Volume I, edited by J. Collins and Peter W. Flint, 91–113. Boston: Brill, 2002.

Krüger, Thomas. "Transformation of History in Ezekiel 20." In *Transforming Visions: Transformations of Text, Tradition, and Theology in Ezekiel*, edited by William A. Tooman and Michael A Lyons, 159–86. Princeton Theological Monograph Series 127. Eugene, OR: Pickwick, 2010.

Laird, Donna. *Negotiating Power in Ezra-Nehemiah*. Ancient Israel and Its Literature 26. Atlanta: SBL, 2016.

Lemaire, André. "Nabonidus in Arabia and Judah in the Neo-Babylonian Period." In *Judah and the Judeans in the Neo-Babylonian Period*, edited by Oded Lipschits and Joseph Blenkinsopp, 285–98. Winona Lake, IN: Eisenbrauns, 2003.

Leveen, Adriane. "Returning the Body to Its Place: Ezekiel's Tour of the Temple." *HTR* 105 (2012) 385–401.

Linafelt, Tod. "The Refusal of a Conclusion in the Book of Lamentations." *JBL* 120 (2001) 340–43.

Lipschits, Oded. "Achaemenid Imperial Policy, Settlement Processes in Palestine, and the Status of Jerusalem in the Middle of the Fifth Century B.C.E." In *Judah and the Judeans in the Persian Period*, edited by Oded Lipschits and Joseph Blenkinsopp, 19–52. Winona Lake, IN: Eisenbrauns, 2006.

———. "Demographic Changes in Judah between the Seventh and the Fifth Centuries B.C.E." In *Judah and the Judeans in the Neo-Babylonian Period*, edited by Oded Lipschits and Joseph Blenkinsopp, 323–76. Winona Lake, IN: Eisenbrauns, 2003.

———. *The Fall and Rise of Jerusalem: Judah under Babylonian Rule*. Winona Lake, IN: Eisenbrauns, 2005.

———. "Shedding New Light on the Dark Years of the 'Exilic Period': New Studies, Further Elucidation, and Some Questions Regarding the Archaeology of Judah as an 'Empty Land.'" In *Interpreting Exile: Interdisciplinary Studies of Displacement and Deportation in Biblical and Modern Contexts*, edited by Brad E. Kelle, Frank Ritchel Ames, and Jacob L. Wright, 57–90. Atlanta: SBL, 2011.

Lipschits, Oded, and Joseph Blenkinsopp, eds. *Judah and the Judeans in the Neo-Babylonian Period*. Winona Lake, IN: Eisenbrauns, 2003.

Lipschits, Oded, Gary N. Knoppers, and Rainer Albertz, eds. *Judah and the Judeans in the Fourth Century B.C.E.* Winona Lake IN: Eisenbrauns, 2007.

Lipschits, Oded, and Manfred Oeming, eds. *Judah and the Judeans in the Persian Period*. Winona Lake, IN: Eisenbrauns, 2006.

Lipschits, Oded, Gary N. Knoppers, and Manfred Oeming, eds. *Judah and the Judeans in the Achaemenid Period: Negotiating Identity in an International Context*. Winona Lake, IN: Eisenbrauns, 2011.

Luc, Alex. "A Theology of Ezekiel: God's Name and Israel's History." *JETS* 26 (1983) 137–43.

Lynch, Matthew J. "Zion's Warrior and the Nations: Isaiah 59:15b—63:6 in Isaiah's Zion Traditions." *CBQ* 70.2 (2008) 244–63.

Maier, Christl M. *Daughter Zion, Mother Zion: Gender, Space and the Sacred in Ancient Israel*. Minneapolis: Fortress, 2008.

Mayes, A. D. H. *The Story of Israel between Settlement and Exile: A Redactional Study of the Deuteronomistic History*. London: SCM, 1983.

McKane, William. *A Critical and Exegetical Commentary on Jeremiah*. Vol. 1. ICC. Edinburgh: T. & T. Clark, 1986.

McKnight, Scot. "Exiled to the Land: N. T. Wright's Exile Theory as Organic to Judaism." In *Exile: A Conversation with N.T. Wright*, edited by James M. Scott, 201–5. Downers Grove, IL: IVP Academic, 2017.

Meyers, Carol L., and Eric M. Meyers. *Zechariah 1–8*. AB 25B. New York: Doubleday, 1987.

Nasuti, Harry P. "A Prophet to the Nations: Diachronic and Synchronic Readings of Jeremiah 1." *HAR* 10 (1986) 249–86.

Nelson, Richard. "The Double Redaction of the Deuteronomistic History: The Case Is Still Compelling." *JSOT* 29 (2005) 319–37.

Neusner, Jacob. "The Idea of History in Rabbinic Judaism: What Kinds of Questions Did the Ancient Rabbis Answer?" *New Blackfriars* 90 (2009) 277–94.

Nguyen, Kim Lan. *Chorus in the Dark: The Voices of the Book of Lamentations*. Hebrew Bible Monographs 54. Sheffield, UK: Sheffield Phoenix, 2013.

Nicholson, E. W. *Preaching to the Exiles: A Study of the Prose Tradition in the Book of Jeremiah*. Oxford: Blackwell, 1967.

Nicholson, Ernest. "Reconsidering the Provenance of Deuteronomy." *ZAW* 124 (2012) 528–40.

Nickelsburg, G. W. E. "The Bible Rewritten and Explained." In *Jewish Writings of the Second Temple Period: Apocrypha, Pseudoepigrapha, Qumran Sectarian Writings, Philo, Josephus*. In *Compendia Rerum Iudaicarum Ad Novum Testamentum. Section Two: The Literature of the Jewish People in the Period of the Second Temple and the Talmud*, edited by Michael E. Stone, 89–156. Assen: Van Gorcum, 1984.

Nilsen, Tina Dykesteen. "The Creation of Darkness and Evil (Isaiah 45:6c–7)." *RB* 115 (2008) 5–25.

Nir, Rivka. *The Destruction of Jerusalem and the Idea of Redemption in the Syriac Apocalypse of Baruch*. SBLEJL 20. Atlanta: SBL, 2003.

Nissinen, Martti. "(How) Does the Book of Ezekiel Reveal Its Babylonian Context." *Die Welt Des Orients* 45 (2015) 85–98.

O'Brien, Mark. *The Deuteronomistic History Hypothesis: A Reassessment*. OBO 92. Freiburg, Schweiz: Universitätsverlag, 1989.

BIBLIOGRAPHY

O'Connor, Kathleen M. *Lamentations and the Tears of the World*. Maryknoll, NY: Orbis, 2002.

Odell, Margaret S. *Ezekiel*. Smyth & Helwys Bible Commentary. Macon, GA: Smyth & Helwys, 2005.

Ollenburger, Ben C. *Zion, The City of the Great King: A Theological Symbol of the Jerusalem Cult*. JSOTSup 41. Sheffield, UK: JSOT, 1987.

Olyan, Saul M. "Purity Ideology in Ezra-Nehemiah as a Tool to Reconstitute the Community." *JSJ* 35 (2004) 1–16.

Parry, Robin A. *Lamentations*. The Two Horizons. Grand Rapids: Eerdmans, 2010.

Pearce, Laurie E. "Identifying Judeans and Judean Identity in the Babylonian Period." In *Exile and Return: The Babylonian Context*, edited by Jonathan Stökl and Caroline Waerzeggers, 7–32. BZAW 478. Berlin: De Gruyter, 2015.

———. "New Evidence for Judeans in Babylonia." In *Judah and the Judeans in the Persian Period*, edited by Oded Lipschits and Manfred Oeming, 399–411. Winona Lake, IN: Eisenbrauns, 2006.

Petersen, David L. *Haggai & Zechariah 1–8*. OTL. London: SCM, 1984.

Piotrowski, Nicholas G. "The Concept of Exile in Late Second Temple Judaism: A Review of Recent Scholarship." *CR:BR* 15 (2017) 214–17.

Pitre, Brant. *Jesus, the Tribulation and the End of the Exile: Restoration Eschatology and the Origin of Atonement*. WUNT 2. Tübingen: Mohr Siebeck; Baker Academic, 2005.

Porten, Bezalel. "Settlement of the Jews at Elephantine and the Arameans at Syene." In *Judah and the Judeans in the Neo-Babylonian Period*, edited by Oded Lipschits and Joseph Blenkinsopp, 451–70. Winona Lake, IN: Eisenbrauns, 2003.

Porten, B. *Archives from Elephantine: The Life of an Ancient Jewish Military Colony*. Berkley: University of California, 1968.

Pritchard, James B., ed. *Ancient Near Eastern Texts Relating to the Old Testament*. Princeton: Princeton University Press, 1955.

Redditt, Paul L. "Daniel 9: Its Structure and Meaning." *CBQ* 62 (2000) 236–49.

Renkema, Johan. *Lamentations*. Leuven: Peeters, 1998.

Rom-Shiloni, Dalit. "Ezekiel as the Voice of the Exiles and Constructor of Exilic Ideology." *HUCA* 76 (2005) 1–45.

———. "Facing Destruction and Exile: Inner-Biblical Exegesis in Jeremiah and Ezekiel." *ZAW* 117 (2005) 189–205.

Rose, Wolter H. "Messianic Expectations in the Early Postexilic Period." In *Yahwism After the Exile: Perspectives on Israelite Religion in the Persian Era*, edited by Rainer Albertz and Bob Becking. STAR 5, 168–85. Assen: Royal Van Gorcum, 2003.

Römer, Thomas. *The So-Called Deuteronomistic History*. London: T. & T. Clark, 2005.

Römer, Thomas, and Albert de Pury. "Deuteronomistic Historiography (DH) History of Research and Debated Issues." In *Israel Constructs Its History*, edited by Albert de Pury, Thomas Römer, and Jean-Daniel Macchi Macchi, 24–141. Sheffield, UK: Sheffield Academic, 2000.

Sack, Ronald H. "Nebuchdnezzar II and the Old Testament: History Versus Ideology." In *Judah and the Judeans in the Neo-Babylonian Period*, edited by Oded Lipschits and Joseph Blenkinsopp, 221–33. Winona Lake, IN: Eisenbrauns, 2003.

Salters, R. B. *Lamentations*. ICC. London: T. & T. Clark, 2010.

Scott, James M., ed. *Exile: A Conversation with N.T. Wright*. Downers Grove, IL: IVP Academic, 2017.

BIBLIOGRAPHY

———, ed. *Exile: Old Testament, Jewish and Christian Conceptions*. JSJSup 56. Leiden: Brill, 1997.

———, ed. *Restoration: Old Testament, Jewish, and Christian Perspectives*. JSJSup 72. Leiden: Brill, 2001.

Sedlmeier, Franz. "The Figure of David and His Importance in Ezekiel 34–37." In *Ezekiel: Current Debates and Future Directions*, edited by William Tooman and Penelope Barter, 92–106. FAT 112. Tübingen: Mohr Siebeck, 2017.

Seow, C. L. *Daniel*. Westminster Bible Companion. Louisville: Westminster John Knox, 2003.

Shead, Andrew. *A Mouth Full of Fire: The Word of God in the Words of Jeremiah*. New Studies in Biblical Theology. Downers Grove, IL: Apollos, 2012.

Smith, Daniel L. "The Politics of Ezra: Sociological Indicators of Postexilic Judaean Society." In *Second Temple Studies: 1. Persian Period*, edited by Philip R. Davies, 73–97. JSOTSup 117. Sheffield, UK: JSOT, 1991.

———. *The Religion of the Landless: The Social Context of the Babylonian Exile*. Bloomington, IN: Meyer-Stone, 1989.

Smith-Christopher, Daniel L. *A Biblical Theology of Exile*. OBT. Minneapolis: Fortress, 2002.

Steck, Odil Hannes. *Das apokryphe Baruchbuch: Studien zu Rezeption und Konzentration kanonisher Überlieferung*. FRLANT 160. Göttingen: Vandenhoeck & Ruprecht, 1993.

Stern, Ephraim. "The Babylonian Gap: The Archaeological Reality." *JSOT* 28.3 (2004) 273–77.

Stevenson, Kalinda Rose. *The Vision of Transformation: The Territorial Rhetoric of Ezekiel 40–48*. SBLDS 154. Atlanta: Scholars, 1996.

Stipp, Hermann-Josef. "The Concept of the Empty Land in Jeremiah 37–43." In *The Concept of Exile in Ancient Israel and Its Historical Contexts*, edited by Ehud Zvi and Christoph Levin, 103–54. BZAW 404. Berlin: De Gruyter, 2010.

———. *Das masoretische und alexandrinische Sondergut des Jeremiabuches: textgeschichtlicher Rang, Eigenarten, Triebkräfte*. OBO 136. Göttingen: Vandenhoeck und Ruprecht, 1994.

Stökl, Jonathan. "'A Youth without Blemish, Handsome, Proficient in All Wisdom, Knowledgeable and Intelligent': Ezekiel's Access to Babylonian Culture." In *Exile and Return: The Babylonian Context*, edited by Jonathan Stökl and Caroline Waerzeggers, 223–52. BZAW 478. Berlin: De Gruyter, 2015.

Stökl, Jonathan, and Caroline Waerzeggers, eds. *Exile and Return: The Babylonian Context*. BZAW 478. Berlin: De Gruyter, 2015.

Strine, C. A. "The Role of Repentance in the Book of Ezekiel: A Second Chance for the Second Generation." *JTS* ns 63 (2012) 467–91.

Talmon, Shemaryahu. "'Exile' and 'Restoration' in the Conceptual World of Ancient Judaism." In *Restoration: Old Testament, Jewish, and Christian Perspectives*, edited by James M. Scott, 107–46. JSJSup 72. Leiden: Brill, 2001.

Thiel, Winfried. *Die Deuteronomistische Redaktion von Jeremia 1–25*. WMANT 41. Neukirchen: Neukirchener, 1973.

Thompson, J. A. *Jeremiah*. NICOT. Grand Rapids: Eerdmans, 1980.

Tuell, Steven S. "Divine Presence and Absence in Ezekiel's Prophecy." In *The Book of Ezekiel: Theological and Anthropological Perspectives*, edited by Margaret S. Odell and John T. Strong, 97–116. SBL Symposium Series 9. Atlanta: SBL, 2000.

BIBLIOGRAPHY

———. "Ezekiel 40–42 as Verbal Icon." *CBQ* 58 (1996) 649–64.

Ulrich, Dean R. *The Antiochene Crisis and Jubilee Theology in Daniel's Seventy Years*. OTS 66. Leiden: Brill, 2015.

Vanderhooft, David. "Babylonian Strategies of Imperial Control in the West: Royal Practice and Rhetoric." In *Judah and the Judeans in the Neo-Babylonian Period*, edited by Oded Lipschits and Joseph Blenkinsopp, 235–62. Winona Lake, IN: Eisenbrauns, 2003.

———. "Cyrus II: Liberator or Conqueror? Ancient Historiography Concerning Cyrus in Babylon." In *Judah and the Judeans in the Persian Period*, edited by Oded Lipschits and Manfred Oeming, 351–72. Winona Lake, IN: Eisenbrauns, 2006.

Wacker, Marie Theres. *Baruch and the Letter of Jeremiah*. Wisdom Commentary. Collegeville, MN: Liturgical, 2016.

Wagner, Thomas. "Die Schuld der Väter (er-)tragen—Thr 5 im Kontext exilischer Theologie." *VT* 62 (2012) 622–35.

Washington, Harold C. "Israel's Holy Seed and the Foreign Women of Ezra-Nehemiah: A Kristevan Reading." *BibInt* 11 (2003) 427–37.

———. "The Strange Woman (הירבנ/הרז השא) of Proverbs 1–9 and Post-Exilic Judaean Society." In *Second Temple Studies: 2. Temple in the Persian Period*, edited by Tamara Eskenazi and Kent Richards, 217–42. JSOTSup 175. Sheffield, UK: Sheffield Academic, 1994.

Westermann, Claus. *Basic Forms of Prophetic Speech*. London: Lutterworth, 1967.

———. *Genesis 1–11: A Commentary*. Minneapolis: Augsburg, 1984.

———. *Genesis 12–36: A Commentary*. Minneapolis: Augsburg, 1985.

———. *Lamentations: Issues and Interpretations*. Edinburgh: T. & T. Clark, 1994.

———. *Praise and Lament in the Psalms*. Atlanta: John Knox, 1978.

Williamson, H. G. M. "Comments on Oded Lipschits *The Fall and Rise of Jerusalem*." *JHS* 7 (2007) art.6, pp. 34–39. Http://www.jhsonline.org/Articles/article_63.pdf.

———. *Ezra, Nehemiah*. WBC 16. Waco, TX: Word, 1985.

Williamson Jr., Robert. "Lament and the Arts of Resistance: Public and Hidden Transcripts in Lamentations 5." In *Lamentations in Ancient and Contemporary Cultural Contexts*, Nancy C. Lee and Carleen Mandolfo, 67–80. SBL Symposium Series 43. Atlanta: SBL, 2008.

Willis, Amy C. Merrill. *Dissonance and the Drama of Divine Sovereignty in the Book of Daniel*. LHBOTS 520. London: T. & T. Clark, 2010.

Wong, Ka Leung. "Profanation/Sanctification and the Past, Present and Future of Israel in the Book of Ezekiel." *JSOT* 28 (2003) 210–39.

Wright, David P. "Holiness in Leviticus and Beyond: Differing Perspectives." *Int* 53 (1999) 351–64.

Wright, J. Edward. *Baruch Ben Neriah: From Biblical Scribe to Apocalyptic Seer*. Columbia SC: University of Carolina Press, 2003.

Wright, N. T. *The New Testament and the People of God*. Christian Origins and the Question of God, Vol. 1. London: SPCK, 1992.

———. "Yet the Sun Will Rise Again: Reflections on the Exile and Restoration in Second Temple Judaism, Paul, and the Church Today." In *Exile: A Conversation with N. T. Wright*, edited by James M. Scott, 19–80. Downers Grove, IL: IVP Academic, 2017.

Zimmerli, Walther. *Ezekiel 1*. Hermeneia. Philadelphia: Fortress, 1979.

———. *I Am Yahweh*. Atlanta: John Knox, 1982.

Zorn, Jeffrey R. "Tell en-Naṣbeh and the Problems of the Material Culture of the Sixth Century." In *Judah and the Judeans in the Neo-Babylonian Period*, edited by Oded Lipschits and Joseph Blenkinsopp, 413–47. Winona Lake, IN: Eisenbrauns, 2003.

AUTHOR INDEX

A

Abraham, Kathleen, 42
Abruyten, Seth, 50
Ackroyd, Peter R., 2, 4, 48, 52
Ahn, John J., 3, 41, 42, 45
Albertz, Rainer, 3, 15, 26, 38, 42, 43, 47, 49, 61, 65, 66, 68, 69
Albright, W. E., 14
Allen, Leslie C., 28, 29, 34, 36, 37, 55, 57
Ames, Frank Ritchel, 41, 45
Amzallag, Nissim, 82, 85
Apóstolo, Silvio, 32
Assis, Elie, 19

B

Baltzar, Klaus, 51
Barstad, Hans M., 13, 15
Bauks, Michaela, 49
Bautch, Richard J., 91,
Beaulieu, Paul-Aland, 42, 67
Becking, Bob, 3, 68
Bedford, Peter R., 66, 71, 72, 76, 77
Ben Ziv, Ehud, 3, 13, 69
Bergsma, John S., 38, 99, 102
Berlin, Adele, 19, 20, 22, 23, 24, 25
Berquist, Jon L., 3
Betylon, John W., 16, 42, 68
Bier, Miriam J., 24
Blenkinsopp, Joseph, 3, 15, 43, 48, 51, 52, 66, 79, 84, 85, 91, 92
Block, Daniel I., 34, 35, 36, 37

Boase, Elizabeth, 20
Boda, Mark J., 3, 42, 74, 75
Boorer, Suzanne, 10, 45
Brettler, Marc Zvi, 46
Briant, Pierre, 65, 67, 68, 85
Bright, John 8, 14
Brueggemann, Walter, 28

C

Campbell, Antony F., 26, 27
Carroll, Robert P., 13, 15, 21, 29, 30
Childs, Brevard S., 47, 48, 51, 53, 91
Clements, Ronald E., 9
Collins, John J., 99, 100, 101, 102, 103
Conrad, Edgar W., 75, 76
Craigie, Peter C., 28, 29
Cross, Frank Moore, 26

D

Dandamayev, M. A., 68
Davies, Philip R., 4
Davis, Ellen F., 32
Davis, Kipp, 116
Delorme, Jean-Philippe, 42
Dimant, Devorah, 105
Dobbs-Allsopp, F. W., 19
Douglas, Mary, 80
Duggan, Michael W., 84
Duhm, Bernhard, 93

AUTHOR INDEX

E

Ehrlich, Carl S., 32

F

Faust, Avraham, 14, 15, 46,
Fishbane, Michael, 101
Foster, R. S., 4
Fried, Lisbeth S., 69, 84, 85, 93
Fritz, Volkmar, 70
Fuller, Michael E., 116

G

Galambush, Julie, 19, 34, 35, 36
Gerstenberger, Erhard S., 43, 68, 72
Gesundheit, Shimon, 93
Goldingay, John E, 98, 99, 100, 101, 102, 103
Goldman, Yohanan, 92
Gregory, Bradley C., 89, 90
Grünwaldt, Klaus, 50

H

Hahn, Scott Walker, 38
Halpern, Baruch, 27
Halvorson-Taylor, Martien, 6
Harris, Beau, 20
Hayes, John H., 42
Hill, John, 29, 30, 44, 69, 93, 94, 95, 96
Holladay, William L., 44

J

Janzen, David, 80, 84
Japhet, Sara, 4, 71, 72, 73, 81, 82
Joyce, Paul M., 32, 34, 35, 54, 55, 56, 57, 59, 60, 61

K

Kelle, Brad E., 3, 58
Keown Gerard L., 44
Kessler, John, 69, 74, 75, 76

Kirkpatrick, Shane, 98
Klein, Anja, 57, 60
Knoppers, Gary N., 3, 70, 75
Koch, Klaus, 97
Körting, Corinna, 75
Kratz, Reinhard, 101
Krüger, Thomas, 37

L

Lemaire, André, 68
Leveen, Adriane, 60, 61
Linafelt, Tod, 25
Lipschits, Oded, 3, 15, 16, 68
Luc, Alex, 32
Lynch, Matthew J., 90

M

Maier, Christl M., 9, 34, 36
Mayes, A. D. H, 11
Mandolfo, Carleen, 20
McKane, William A., 29
McKnight, Scot, 116
Meyers, Carol L., 73
Meyers, Eric M., 73

N

Nasuti, Harry P., 21
Nelson, Richard, 26
Neusner, Jacob, 117
Nguyen, Kim Lan, 25
Nicholson, E. W., 11, 29, 30, 31
Nickelsburg, G. W. E, 105
Nilsen, Tina Dyksteen, 51
Nir, Rivka, 116
Nissinen, Martti., 42

O

O'Brien, Mark, 26, 27, 70
O'Connor, Kathleen, 19, 23
Odell, Margaret S., 34, 35
Ollenburger, Ben C., 9
Olyan, Saul M., 80

AUTHOR INDEX

P

Parry, Robin A., 25
Pearce, Laurie E., 42
Petersen, David L., 73, 75
Piotrowski, Nicholas G., 2, 116
Pitre, Brant., 114
Porten, Bezalel, 69
Pritchard, James B., 65

R

Redditt, Paul L., 102
Renkema, Johan, 24, 25
Rom-Shiloni, Dalit, 33, 37, 38, 55
Rose, Wolter H., 73
Römer, Thomas, 26, 27

S

Sack, Ronald H., 16
Salters, R. B, 25
Scott, James M., 3, 4
Sedlmeier, Franz., 61
Seow, C. L., 99, 101, 102
Shead, Andrew A., 92, 96
Smith(-Christohpher), Daniel L., 3, 42, 43, 80,
Steck, Odil Hannes, 107, 108
Stern, Ephraim, 14
Stevenson, Kalinda Rose, 60, 61
Stipp, Hermann-Josef, 13, 92
Stökl, Jonathan, 3, 42, 43
Strine C. A., 37

T

Talmon, Shemaryahu, 69, 70, 72, 73
Thiel, Winfried, 29, 30
Thompson, J. A., 44, 94
Tuell, Steven S., 60, 61

U

Ulrich, Dean R., 101

V

Vanderhooft, David, 14, 16, 42, 65

W

Wacker, Marie Teres, 105, 107
Wagner, Thomas, 24
Washington, Harold C., 80
Westermann, Claus, 22, 24, 46, 49
Williamson, H. G. M., 79
Williamson Jr., 24, 71
Willis, Amy C., 98
Wong, Ka Leung, 38
Wright, David P., 12
Wright, J. Edward, 104, 105, 116
Wright, N. T., 3, 111, 114,

Z

Zimmerli, Walther, 56
Zorn, Jeffrey R., 16, 68

BIBLICAL INDEX

OLD TESTAMENT

Genesis

1:1—2:4a	45, 46
1:2	45
1:4	46
1:6–7	46
2	94
2:2–3	45
2:15	94
10:10	75
11–17	35
11:1–3	75, 98
11:1–9	98
12:1–9	10
12:6–9	10
12:14	10
17	40, 49
26:24	94

Exodus

5:1	29
12:21–23	50
12:33–34	53
14:19	53
20:10	46
34:6	22

Leviticus

5:5	106
10:10	47
11:46	47
18:24–25	12
20:22	12
25	103
25:8	101
25:10	90
26:32–35	4
26:34–43	12
26:40	106

Numbers

5:7	106
12:7	94
14	35

Deut

4:29	108
4:34	91
5:12–15	46
7:1–3	80
7:2	35
16:1–7	50
23:1–3	80
23:3	80
26:9	28
28:53	102
28:55	102
28:57	102
29:24–25	30

BIBLICAL INDEX

2 Samuel

7:1–17	10
7:5	94
7:8	94

1 Kings

8:46–51	70
8:48	70
9:8	30

2 Kings

17	35
18–20	9
19:33–34	9
21:2	27
21:3	27
21:5	27
21:7	27
21:21	27
23:25	27
24:2	27
24:10–17	11
24:13–17	77
24:14	11
25	11
25:5–7	12
25:8	105
25:9	12
25:11–12	12
25:13–17	12
25:18	72
25:21	12, 27

1 Chronicles

3:19	72
6:14	72
6:15	72

2 Chronicles

35:2–7	11
36:17–21	77
36:20	13
36:21	4, 12
36:22–23	13
36:22	77, 81
36:23	77

Ezra

1	13
1:1	77, 81, 99
1:2–3	77
1:3	69
1:7–11	77
2	77, 112
2:1	72
3	77
4:1	77
6:16–18	77
7	80, 82
7:1–3	80
7:3	78
8:1–34	78
8:36	73
9–10	79, 80
9	83, 84
9:1–3	78
9:1	80
9:2	78, 80
9:4	78
9:8	85
9:9	84
9:13–15	85
9:16	100
10	78, 82
10:44	78

Nehemiah

1:1	82
1:2	85
1:3	83
1:5–11	100
1:6	106
2–4	80, 82
2:7	73
2:9	73
4:1–23	82
5	82

BIBLICAL INDEX

6–7	80, 82
6:1–19	92
7:6	84
8	80
8:1	82
8:9	82
8:12	82
8:14–18	82
9	83
9:2	83, 85, 106
9:6–31	84
9:32–37	84
9:6–37	83
10	84
10:3	83
10:32	84
10:36–37	84
11–13	83
11:25–26	85
13:23–27	85

Psalms

48:1–2	9
48:4–5	9

Isaiah

10:5	93
13–14	93
20:3	94
40–55	5, 6, 43, 48, 49, 50, 51, 53, 66, 88, 89, 90, 91, 92, 108, 109, 112, 115
40–48	51
40:1–11	51
40:1	52, 90, 91, 116
40:3	115, 116
40:4	108
40:9	52, 89
40:11	51
40:12–31	51
40:15	51
40:18	51
40:22	51
40:27	43, 51
43:5	108
43:13	91
43:18–19	91
44:9–20	47, 48
44:20	48
44:1–8	47
44:19	47
44:24—45:8	51
44:24–28	51
44:24	51
44:25	51
44:26	51, 90
44:28	51
45	52
45:1	51
45:5–8	52
45:9–13	52
46:1–2	48
46:3–4	48
46:4	48
46:1–7	48
46:6–7	48
46:7	48
46:8–13	48
46:9	48
46:13	48
47:1–6	47
49:13	90
49:14–21	90
49:14	43, 90, 108, 109
49:15–21	90
49:18	108
49:19	90
50:2	43
51	52, 53
51:1–2	53
51:2	90
51:9–11	52
51:9–13	52
51:10–11	52
51:12	90
52	52
52:1–3	89
52:1	108
52:7	52, 89
52:8	89
52:9	52, 90, 99, 100
52:11–13	89
54:1–3	91

BIBLICAL INDEX

Nehemiah *(continued)*

54:4	106
56–66	6, 88, 91, 92, 108, 112, 116, 117
56:1–3	91
59	91
60–62	89
60:3	108
61:1–3	89, 90, 91
61:1	89, 90, 116
61:2	90
61:3	90,
61:4	90
61:10	108
63:17—64:12	91
64:8–12	92
64:8	92
64:12	91, 92, 112
65:17	91
65:21–23	45

Jeremiah

1:1–3	96
1:2–3	95
2–6	28
2:2–3	28
2:3	28
2:6–7	28
2:7	28
2:24	30
2:26	28, 30, 106
2:32	28
4:3	28
4:22–27	45
4:23–26	96
4:23	45
4:27	96
5:19	30
6:13	30
8:1	28
9:11–15	30
9:12	31
9:26	46
11:2	28
11:9	28
13:13	28
13:25	28
14:1	29
14:14–18	30
14:18	30
15:1–4	29
16–17	96
16:10–13	30
16:10	31
16:11	31
16:14–15	96
17	55
17:10	55
17:12–21	55
17:17–24	55
17:22–24	55
17:23	55
17:25	28
18:11	28
18:15	28
21:2	10
21:5–6	93
21:7	94
21:1—23:8	29
22:8–9	30
22:8	31
22:11–22	29
22:18–23	29
22:19	30
22:24–30	29
22:24–28	73
22:24	73
23	30
23:14	30
23:17	30
24	12, 13
24:8	69
25	94
25:1–14	94
25:15–29	94
29:15–26	94
25:9	94
25:11	12, 77, 100
25:11–12	99, 100
25:17	95
25:26	95
25:29	94
26–36	96
26:24	69

27	94
27:1–3	94
27:5–6	94
27:6	94
28	44
28:3	30, 44
29–33	96
29	44
29:4–7	40, 44, 67
29:5–7	45
29:7	44
29:10	12, 77, 99, 100
31:19–20	107
31:33	55
32:32	28
36	29
36:23	30
36:25	30
36:27–31	96
36:30	30
39:1–7	12
39:8	12
39:1–10	11, 12
39:14	69
40–43	12
40:2–3	30, 31
40:5	69
40:7–13	13
41:1–3	13
42:1–3	13
42:6	13
42:17	13
43–44	69
43:18	69
44:9	19
46–51	96
50–51	93
52	96
52:1–11	95
52:4–30	11
52:9–11	11
52:13	12
52:15–16	12
52:17–23	12, 77
52:27	12
52:28	11
52:31–34	95

Lamentations

1	21
1:1–11b	19
1:2	19
1:5	19
1:7	20
1:8	19
1:12	19
1:11c–22	19
1:14	20
1:15	20
1:18	20
1:19	20
1:21	20
1:22	19, 20
2	21
2:1–10	20
2:1	20
2:2	20
2:3	20
2:5	20
2:11–19	20
2:15	20
2:17	20
2:20–22	20
2:20	21
3	21
3:1–10	23
3:4	23
3:5	23
3:10	23
3:12	23
3:13	23
3:1–16	23
3:17–22	23
3:17–20	23
3:20	23
4	23
4:1–11	23
4:1	24
4:11	23
4:13	23
4:21–22	23
5	24
5:1	24, 83
5:2–3	24
5:2–18	24

BIBLICAL INDEX

5:4–10	24	17:24	53
5:7	24	18:2	107
5:11–13	24	20	37
5:14–18	24	20:1–4	37
5:16	24	20:1	37, 43
5:19	24	20:5–44	37
5:20–22	24, 25	20:5–31	37
5:20	24, 25	20:5–9	37
5:21	24, 25	20:6–7	37
5:22	25, 38, 41, 92, 112	20:9	38
		20:10–17	37
		20:14	38

Ezekiel

		20:18–26	37
		20:22	38
1:1	32	20:25	38
1:2	32–33	20:32–44	37
2:1	33	20:40–44	54, 55, 56
3:1	33	20:62	55, 56
5:14, 15	33, 83	20:63	55
8–11	14, 59	23	36
8:1	43	23:4	36
11:1–13	54	23:5–21	36
11:14–21	54	23:17	36
11:15	33, 54	23:22–35	36
11:16–21	54	23:37–39	36
11:17	54	33:20	57
11:19–20	54	33:21	33, 57
11:21	33	33:23–29	57
14:1	43	33:24	33
16	34	34	57
16:3–34	34	34:8	57
16:3	34	34:9–16	57
16:4–6	33	34:20–31	57
16:6–34	36	34:23	57, 58
16:8–14	35	34:26–29	57
16:15–34	35	34:30–31	58
16:17–18	35	36	58
16:21	35	36:20	58
16:22–43	36	36:21–22	58
16:36, 37	106	36:28	59
16:44	35	37:1–14	59
16:46	35	37:4–8	59
16:48	36	37:11–14	59
16:51–52	35–36	37:11	59
16:52	36	37:15–28	59
16:59–63	54, 55, 56	37:23	59
16:62	53	37:24	60
17:22–24	54	37:25	60

BIBLICAL INDEX

39:28	53
40–48	60, 61
40:1	33
40:2	71
40:3	60
40:5—42:20	60
42:20	61
43:1–12	60
43:3	61
43:5	60
43:7	60
43:8–12	60
44	60
44:6–14	60
44:5	62
44:9	62
45:1–8	61
46:2–18	61
48	61
48:8	61
48:21	61
48:35	62

Daniel

1–4	113
1:1–2	97–98
1:1	97
1:21	98
6:1	99
9:1	99
9	99, 100, 102, 103
9:2	97, 100, 113
9:3–19	100
9:3	100
9:5–11	113
9:7	100, 106
9:8	100
9:16	100
9:19	101
9:20–27	101
9:23–24	101
9:25	102
9:27	103
10:1	99

Haggai

1:1	71, 73
1:2	71
1:4	71
1:5–6	72
2:3	71
2:6	72
2:21	72

Zechariah

1–8	70
1:4–6	76
1:4	74
1:11	74
1:12	74
1:17	76
1:18–21	74
2:4–5	76
2:7	75
2:8	76
2:12	76
3	75
5:5–11	75
5:11	98
6:10	75
7:8–14	74, 76
8:6	76
8:7	74
8:13	76
8:14	76
8:20–22	76

NEW TESTAMENT

Matthew

3:3	115
1:2	115
1:11	115
1:16	115
1:17	115
11:1–6	116

Mark

1:3	115

Luke

3:4	115
2:25	116

APOCRYPHA

Baruch

1:1–15	105
1:1	105
1:2	105
1:3	105
1:10	106
1:11–12	106
1:13	106
1:14	106
1:15—3:8	100, 105
1:15	106
1:19–21	107
2:6	106
3:5	107
3:7–8	107
3:8	107, 108
3:9—4:4	105, 108
3:9—5:9	105
4:9–37	108
4:36–37	108
4:37	108
5:1–9	108
5:1	108
5:3	108
5:5	108
5:7	108

www.ingramcontent.com/pod-product-compliance
Lightning Source LLC
Chambersburg PA
CBHW022127160426
43197CB00009B/1185